Gods and Goddesses of India: 6

LAKSHMI

B. K. Chaturvedi

bfa
BOOKS FOR ALL
Delhi - 110052

Sales Office:
D.K. Publishers Distributors (P) Ltd.
1. Ansari Road, Darya Ganj.
New Delhi-110 002
Phone : 3261465, 3278368
Fax : 091-011-3264368

© 1996 Publisher
1996 B.K. Chaturvedi (b 1945—)
ISBN 81-7386-146-3

All rights, including the right to translate or to reproduce this book or parts thereof except for brief quotations, are reserved.

Published by:
Books For All
A-6, Nimri Commercial Centre
Near Bharat Nagar, Ashok Vihar
Delhi-110 052.
Phone : 7452453
Fax : 091-011-7138265

Laser Typeset by:
Ideal Printers, Delhi-110 007

Printed at:
D.K. Fine Art Press (P) Ltd., Delhi-110 052

PRINTED IN INDIA

Introduction

Goddess Lakshmi is the unique deity in the Hindu pantheon who grants all material wealth and riches to her devotees. Since the material wealth and worldly riches occupy most degraded position in the normal desires of a devout devotee—in conformity with our religious tenets, her getting this exalted position and becoming the spouse of the most revered god, Lord Vishnu, appears, on prima facie viewing, a contradiction in terms. Why should a race deriding material wealth have a deity bestowing all those things which are deemed evil in scores of scriptural accounts? How and why Lakshmi came to be associated with material wealth and worldly prosperity and what made this concept gain acceptances are some of the questions that have been tackled with a view to provide a logical answer. Since not much material is available on this unique goddess in even mythological accounts barring her casual references here and there, most of the interpretations mentioned in the book are based on the various religious, social and even domestic practices prevalent in our society from the hoary past. In order to assess the social status of this goddess we have also culled a few folk tales doing rounds perpetually in many parts of our country. This is done precisely to present a full picture of the goddess's personality before our lay but awakened reader. All the famous hymns, orisons, prayers etc., have also been given in the end of the book with their texts in Nagari and Roman scripts alongwith the minimum possible and relevant diacritical marks to help the reader get their correct pronunciation, and their English and Hindi prose renderings. Some of these prayers are in colloquial parlance whose authenticity could be suspected but their extreme popularity among certain sections of our society advocates strongly in favour of their inclusion in the book.

It is perhaps the only book which contains all the mythological, social, cultural and even folk references about the goddess in one volume. The interpretations herein are given purely from the logical angle without any religious prejudices and predilections. May the goddess shed her grace upon the readers, publishers and of course on the author of the book in equal measure!

Lastly the author wishes to convey his gratitude to 'Books for All' for giving him a free hand to write about the goddess without any inhibition.

—B.K. Chaturvedi

Contents

Introduction ... iii

1. Goddess Lakshmi: The Churned Out Gem from the Ocean ... 1
2. Lakshmi: The Goddess of Wealth and Prosperity ... 7
3. Goddess Lakshmi: In Various Mythological Legends ... 26
   (i) Goddess Lakshmi's Incarnation as Tulsi (Basil Plant) ... 26
   (ii) Goddess Lakshmi's Incarnation as a Mare ... 30
   (iii) Goddess Lakshmi's Role in Demon Jalandhar's Episode ... 31
   (iv) Goddess Lakshmi's Worship by Indra ... 37
   (v) Yuddhishthir's Performing Goddess Lakshmi's Worship on the Advice of Lord Krishna ... 40
4. Goddess Lakshmi: In Folk Tales of India. ... 44
   (i) The Prudent Old Woman ... 44
   (ii) The Komati Way ... 48
   (iii) Goddess Lakshmi's Promise ... 49
   (iv) Goddess Lakshmi Curtails Lord Vishnu's Sleep ... 53
   (v) Goddess Lakshmi: A Deity Kind to the Humble ... 56
5. The Ritualistic Worship of Goddess Lakshmi ... 63

6.	Famous Temples of Goddess Lakshmi	68
	(i) Lakshmi Narayan Temple, Delhi	68
	(ii) Lakshmi Narain Temple, Mathura-Vrindavan	68
	(iii) Lakshmi Narain Temple, Jaipur	68
	(iv) Lakshmi Narayan Temple, Ellora Caves	69
	(v) Mahalakshmi Temple, Bombay	69
7.	लक्ष्मी देवी की प्रसिद्ध स्तुतियाँ, श्लोक, प्रार्थनाएं, आरती इत्यादि (नागरी व रोमन लिपि में मूल पाठ एवम् हिन्दी-अंग्रेजी में अनुवाद सहित)	72
	Some Famous and Popular Hymns, Orisons, Ārtis etc., of Goddess Lakshmi (With Their Romanised Text Versions and Hindi-English Translations)	
	(i) महालक्ष्म्यष्टकम्	72
	Eight Verses of Eulogy for Goddess Lakshmi	
	(ii) देव्या आरात्रिकम्	78
	The Evening Invocation of the Goddess	
	(iii) श्री लक्ष्मी चालीसा	82
	Forty Rhymes in the Honour of Goddess Lakshmi	
	(iv) श्री लक्ष्मी जी की आरती	100
	Ārti of Goddess Lakshmi	

(Lakshmi)

1. Goddess Lakshmi: The Churned Out Gem from the Ocean

It is mentioned in the Puranas that whole of our creation originated from sage Kashyap's physical contact with the thirteen daughters of Daksha Prajāpati who were married to the sage. His first two wives were Aditi and Diti. Aditi was the mother of all gods and Diti of all demons. Gods and demons represent the positive and negative aspects of human life. Although born of the same father, the sage Kashyap, these two races were all the time fighting with each other. But being physically more powerful, the demons always managed to defeat the gods. At last, to find solution to their problem, the gods went to Brahma who expressed his inability to offer them any permanent solution but took them to Vishnu who was believed to be the most brilliant among all the gods. Lord Vishnu suggested that they should churn the ocean which contained many gems including nectar. If the gods could imbibe nectar they would become immortal and hence invincible by the demons. But how to churn the mighty ocean? Lord Vishnu said they should have a powerful rope and a huge churner. Also, a base was needed to place the churner upon. Lord Vishnu agreed to provide the base and he immediately incarnated himself as a mighty tortoise. The gods managed to make the huge mount Mandarachal agree to become the churner. Receiving the request from the gods the Serpent Shesh[1] uprooted the Mount Mandarachal. Another serpent, Vasuki, consented to become the rope as it was most sturdy among all the snakes. But when the demons learnt about gods' attempt to churn the ocean to get the nectar they also agreed to help the gods provided they received half of the nectar as their share. Since the effort was to be very strenuous the gods felt that

---
1. According to mythology the whole world rests on its 1,000 hoods.

owing to the great physical power of the demons, their help would be a great relief to them.

At last the preparations were complete and they began the churning operation. The clever gods held the serpent Vasuki–their churning rope–from the tail side while his hood was clutched by the demons. Now with great force they began to churn the ocean. Owing to the great stress toxic fumes began to issue from the mouth of the serpent, distressing the demons. As the gods' good luck would have it, those massive fumes soon turned into clouds which rained cool water and brought relief to them. Though this churning lasted for quite a long time, nothing arose from the sea. The gods began to lose their heart. But Lord Vishnu asked them to be patient and start the operation with redoubled vigour.

At long last their efforts began to bear fruit and the precious things began to emerge from the ocean. As milk is churned to receive butter from it, so was the ocean churned and it produced fourteen precious articles. How these were distributed is explained below.

First to emerge was Surabhi, (or Kāmdhenu), the cow of abundance which was given to seven lower-status gods (Vasus). Next to come was Varuni or Sura which the demons received. Then came the celestial tree 'Paarijata,' (or the Kalpa Vriksha) the tree which fulfils every desire. This was planted by gods' chief Indra in his garden. Rambha, the Apsara (the divine danseuse) who became the progenitor of all apsaras, was next to come, followed by Chandra (the moon) which emerged casting his cool rays. Shiv took it and adorned it on his head. Kaustubha, the most precious stone emerged and it was taken by Vishnu. Airāvat, the winged elephant emerged next and Indra took it as his mount. Uchchaishrava, the white horse with a black tail, on its emergence, was taken by the demon-king Bāli. Then out emerged the Shankh (Conch) which Lord Vishnu took in his possession. The divine physician, called Dhanvantari was next to emerge, holding the pitcher of nectar in his hands. As nectar emerged the demon leapt to take possession of it but Vishnu, who had assumed the form of an enchantress or Mohini, prevented them and all the gods insisted on completing the operation,[2] for seeing the things emerging they grew slightly avaricious and did not want to leave anything precious lying in the ocean. When Kaal-koot (the deadly poison) emerged there was no taker. At last all requested Shiv to have its as only he was capable of withstanding its toxic effect. Though Shiv drank it, he did not let it go down his throat. But owing to its severe toxicity his throat had turned blue. Goddess Lakshmi was the last to emerge and she was immediately taken by Vishnu as his consort. Lakshmi was seated on a lotus and looked so beautiful that everyone sang her praises, the sky-elephants (Diggaj[3]) poured refreshing waters from the Ganga on her and the Ocean of Milk gave her a garland of imperishable flowers.

Meanwhile, the demon continued to be enchanted by Lord Vishnu's Mohini form. The Lord tried to impress upon the demons that if nectar was imbibed by the gods first, the latter would receive only the surface part of the divine potion while the real essence of nectar would remain reserved for the demons. The demons were already under the hypnotic spell of the Mohini. So they agreed to let the gods imbibe it first.

While Vishnu's spell was on, a demon, Rahu, son of the demoness Sinhika, saw through Vishnu's game and joined the gods' queue for drinking nectar early. Vishnu did not notice this but his espouse, Lakshmi, had seen Rahu's coming over to the gods' queue in a disguised form. By this time Vishnu had poured nectar down Rahu's throat. At that very moment Lakshmi pointed out the deceit Rahu had played on them and Vishnu,

---

2. Different mythological sources give different order of their emergence. Some say nectar emerged the last while some say it was Lakshmi.

3. Mythologically it is believed that while whole of the earth is supported on the hood of the Shesh and the Tortoise, the four directions are further balanced by four mighty elephants, each from one direction.

immediately hacked off Rahu's head with his discus. But since nectar had reached upto Rahu's throat, the demon was not dead despite being beheaded. His head and trunk independently remained alive.

Some mythological accounts, however, say that Rahu's deceit was first noticed by the luminary gods, the Sun and the Moon, who immediately beckoned at Rahu and told Vishnu about the deceit. Since Vishnu was busy holding the pitcher of nectar, he asked Lakshmi to hack off Rahu's head. Lakshmi did so without delay. But the demon had his head and trunk independently alive. The head came to be known as Rahu or the Dragon's Head and the trunk, the Dragon's Tail, came to be known as Ketu.[4] Since then the moon and the sun became permament enemy of Rahu and Ketu respectively. It is held mythologically that at the time of lunar eclipse, it is Rahu which overshadows the moon and in solar eclipse the sun is shadowed by Ketu.

The moment Vishnu finished pouring nectar down the gods throat, he discarded his Mohini form and came in his original form. Then taking his discus he began to fight with the demons. The gods, after imbibing nectar, had, even otherwise, became quite powerful. So together, they defeated the demons decisively. The demon had no go but to flee and hide themselves in various caves and in the nether world or Pataal. All the things that were used in the sea-churning were restored to their original position and Vishnu also retired to his couch made of the coils of the Serpent Sheshnag.

At last all was well. Indra sang a hymn of praise to Lakshmi[5] and she was so pleased that she promised never to forsake anyone

---

4. This explanation appears more logical in the light of the modern astronomical researches which say that Rahu is the nodal point at the Moon-Earth's axis while Ketu at the Sun-Earth's axis. Moreover an ancient Verse Praising Lakshmi eulogises her hacking off the head of Rahu which is given in the Hymn's section of the Book.

5. The same with original text and translations is given in the 'Hymn Section' of the book.

who sang Indra's hymn to her. It is held that this hymn is very effective even today and those who want prosperity sing it every day.

Lakshmi has various names : Shree, Indira, Kamalā, Lokmātā, Jaladhijā (born of the ocean), Hari priya (beloved of Lord Vishnu) etc. Each of these names in a sort of adjective to describe the person of Lakshmi. Born seated on the lotus flower, she is Padmā. She has always appeared as Vishnu's life partner in every incarnation of his. When Vishnu came on earth as Vaman (the Dwarf) Lakshmi came to earth as a Lotus (Padma or Kamala); when he came as Parashurām, Lakshmi assumed the form of his wife, Dharini. She came to the mortal world as Sita when Vishnu appeared as Rām. In Krishna incarnation she is said to have incarnated herself as Radha or Satyabhama. She is called 'Chanchala' because of fortune's fickle nature, for, as the providence has willed, no one can bask in the shine of favourable fortune all through one's life.

How she came to be recognised as the goddess of prosperity has been dealt at length in the coming chapter. Her this position is determined more by psychological reasons than by mythological legends. In mythology, whenever she is associated with some part of the body of a person, she grants different gifts. It is said that when she stays at the feet, she bestows the gift of a house, when on thighs she gives wealth; when in the bosom she gives a lucky child; when in the genitals, a very lucky wife; when on the heart, she grants the fulfilment of wishes; when around the neck, she ensures one's meeting with loved ones or with lost relatives, and when in the face, the goddess bestows beauty and grace. This belief is more borne by worldly considerations and so in the other words it can be said that when one gets the above mentioned things it means the Goddess is staying with the person at the various positions of his body.

The abode of Lakshmi is said to be ocean where she stays on the serpent Shesh's coil alongwith her husband Vishnu.

Vishnu's choosing to stay in his wife's abode led many medieval Hindi poets remark epigrammatically that "Even Vishnu has to become a 'Ghar Jamai,' in his yearning to live with the goddess of prosperity." Another remarked "Purush purātan kee vadhoo kyon na chanchalā hoi?" Meaning, why shouldn't the wife of an old man be fickle? This remark is more apt looking to the basic fickle nature of fortune and the primal status of Lord Vishnu who is said to be the source of all creation.

The moon is said to be brother of Lakshmi because both had their origin in the ocean.

Goddess Lakshmi is personified as not only the goddess of fortune and wealth but also as an embodiment of loveliness, grace and charm. She is normally depicted seated on a lotus. In her pictures gold coins are seen dropping down from the palms of this goddess of prosperity.

This goddess is sometimes represented with four arms but more often with two. She has no temple exclusively devoted to her but always appears as a consort of Vishnu. Still she is regularly worshipped in every shop and home—specially on Deepavali day alongwith Lord Ganesh in almost all Hindu business houses. Some times Lakshmi is also shown as being one with Lord vishnu and their combined image is called Lakshmi-Narayan. This conjoined deity denotes that in his supreme state Vishnu is one with his consort, who represents his power and energy.

---

6. The bride groom who stays at his wife's parental house.

2. Lakshmi: The Goddess of Wealth and Prosperity

Normally all the deities of the Hindu pantheism acquire their exalted positions on the support of various legends describing their supernal feats. But Goddess Lakshmi is one of the exceptions. There is no legend glorifying Lakshmi's any such doing. Her eternal Spouse, Vishnu, by scores of his such doings has assumed almost Supreme Being Status for the Hindu devout. He incarnated Himself frequently to subdue or kill the demonic forces that threatened to disturb the very order of the world. He always comes for the rescue of the gods. The same way we have innumerable legends to justify the exalted status of Lord Shiv, Goddess Durga and even the secondary gods like Hanuman or Ganesh. But no such legend is available for Goddess Lakshmi. No doubt that the deity is not a person like we beings are. It is a force, an urge, an impulse a necessity and an aspiration. But having put these divinities on the exalted pedestal, human logical mind wove many legends in conformity with its own aspirations. Man created god whenever he found some lacunae in his logical observation. When it was impossible to fly, he created the wind-god. When keeping a tiny lamp lighted was impossible he made the luminaries like the Moon and the Sun his gods. As a matter of fact the entire pantheism is man's creation in his different levels of advancement. For a modern man a god would be he who cures, AIDS, removes cancerous growths etc. In short what is beyond his power is god. And once he has identified the force or energy which he wished he could have, he began to humanise his concept of that force. So he began to give his gods a family and mannerisms according to the maximum stretch of his imagination. Though his god be just a force, he has his favourite weapon, favourite food, favourite mounts like we humans have. The Rig Veda describes the glory in the prayers for many solar deities : Mitra, Surya, Savitri, Pushan, Bhag etc., which are all personification of certain functions of the sun. The aura of divinity is cast only after having identified the force or energy that meets the human aspiration. Thus every effort is made to justify the Gods we worship. But surprisingly no such glorification by way of weaving legends or events was ever made with regard to goddess Lakshmi. She just emerged out of the ocean and became the wife of the God adored most by his fellow gods and men. And not only this, she immediately became the goddess of all prosperity and wealth. Nowhere it is mentioned that why this goddess was accorded such an important divine 'portfolio'. What made her the goddess of all those things the humans aspire for most?

Before tackling such questions we would have to delve deep into the ancient Hindu psyche. This faith, though erroneously referred to as the Hindu Dharma, is that belief which is based upon the solid foundation of logic. Weaving legends around some scientific fact to accord it a divine hue has been the speciality of the Sanatan Dharma. Sanatan Dharma is the faith the erroneously called Hindus adhere to. Literal meaning of this is perennial duty or the perpetual code of conduct. But for whom? It is for all beings, for those that wish to preserve life on this planet. The ancients summarised the essence of their experience and gave this code. None of this faith's tenets is without any empirical wisdom. All rituals, all festivals and all the principles enshrine some basic fact of life. This tendency is quite apparent in the ancient scriptures of the same faith, which are full of symbols, analogies, allegories and so on. The words and expressions that are used are nothing but the images and symbols shaped through abstract mental equivalents of one's directly apprehended experiences with external environments. The authors of such scriptures looked at Nature comprehensibly, both at her outer physical phenomenon and her inner invisible psyche. The symbols they invariably used for expressing the invisible by means of visible. Like we coined words to express our inner feelings, they devised symbols to communicate their subtle psychological feelings and experiences. They used these symbols to explain infinite by means of finite. Those who gave the concept of 'nothingness' or zero also knew how to create something out of nothing. Geometry offers a fine example to explain this process. A point is defined as having no magnitude. But by points we make lines which has length, by lines we create two dimensional figures and by these figures, the World! Thus these allegories and symbols which prima facie may appear meaningless have as much relevance as the nothingness of the point to create the world. The same is true with the allegories and stories woven round a big scientific fact. The story of the 'Churning of the Ocean' is one such allegory which is also woven round a commonly occurring natural phenomenon. But if we analyse this big event on the relevance of our own experience we would appreciate it better.

Water has been accorded the greatest importance by the ancient thinkers out of all the five constituent elements of the Creation. We also know how important water is for the growth and preservation of life. Whenever our astronomers and astrophysicists search for any sign of life in other planets and galaxies they invariably search for water first. For life is only possible with water. Water not only breeds life, it helps in its growth and preservation also. Water is the source of life.

Moreover, in the tropical country like India or the climes of the Indian subcontinent, water assumes still greater importance. The hot and humid conditions make water an indispensible necessity of life. Hence the supreme importance of rivers in our life. No other country in the world gives these rivers the status of the mother. "Ganga Maiyya Ki Jai", "Jai Narmada Maiyya" are the regular chants one hear on the banks of these sacred rivers. The importance of water in all our religious rituals is explained by this reason only. Not only in the religious festivals but even in the obsequies and the ceremonies after death of the person, water is offered to the departed souls. This ritual had led Shahjehan, the Mughal Emperor, to remark in his missive to his disobedient son, Aurangjeb, that "how fortunate are those whose progeny offer them water even after their death while you, my own son, has stopped the supply of water to me even when I am alive." For the Hindus or the Sanatan Dharmis, one accrues maximum divine merit to one's final account by offering water to the thirsty.

In this context it is interesting to note that one of the most popular epithets of Lord Vishnu is 'Narayan', which literally means "he who has his abode in water," or "water is whose abode". Maybe owing to his this speciality he is accorded the most exalted position in the Hindu Pantheism. One of the popular hymn of the Rig Veda requests the chief of the gods, Indra, that "he who pollutes my water may be slain by your thunderbolt."

All these factors indicate the reason of extraordinary importance given to water in the Sanatan Dharmic thought. But while water is the source and protector of life, its excess can lead to Pralaya or the Final Dissolution when everything gets submerged and the whole world is just a vast body of water. The concept of Pralaya is not a unique aspect of ancient Indian thought's powerful imagination but it is also available in the scores of scriptural books of the other races. This Pralaya is a phenomenon that takes place to signify the end of one cycle of the four ages called : Satya, Treta, Dwaper and Kaliyug. Before its advent the sun becomes very scorching, melting all the snow in the world. Then those vapours become clouds to rain down water again to overwhelm the earth. The onset of Pralaya is very vividly described by the ace modern Hindi poet Jaishankar Prasad in his immortal classic 'Kamayani'. The author of this book has also translated this classic whose relevant piece describing the Pralaya is quoted below.

"That wailing uproar, grim thunderbolts smashed
Horizons deafened, rowdy-notes cruelly banged and crashed
Smoke of the horizons' fire, or rose clouds from the globe's end
Quacking the space entire, all typhoons seemed loosened.

Sink sallow sun in the dark, ceased splendours to spark;
Varuna busy, thick to thicker, was solidifying dark,
Five Elements grisly fusion, ceaseless falls of lightning
Meteors with the unfading power, as if search lost morning

Quacked in those thundering gales, beholding poor earth's plight
As if sympathy made, to embrace welkin alight!
There roaring sea's billows, like Time's wicked snares
Excreting froth coming, like vipers hood in flares!

Earth sinking, flaring flames, exhaling volcanoes;
Contracting limbs of the earth, decaying gradually low
Furious seas's gruesome waves' assaults made the earth distressed
Like a big tortoise it was, greatly turmoiled perplexed

Like luxury's rapacity, increased that eerie rain
Fluid dark! Deluging gales, entwined in a unity chain
Every moment came nearer the shores, horizons grew dim disappeared
Sea having sunk full earth, all fetters it had cleared
Thundering lightnings roared and crushed all that lay below
Five Elements's Tandav Dance—had a very long go !"

The piece describes the grisly spectacle of Pralaya. All that was existent on the earth became dissolved in water. Implied by this means that all the gems of the earlier civilisation or culture get lost in water. Even the earth itself looses its existence. When the conditions become normal and earth emerges out of water the attempt is made to retrieve the precious gems or the creations of the earlier cycle. That was the attempt made by the demons and the gods—the survivors of the previous cycle—when they churned the ocean on Lord Vishnu's advice. So Lakshmi represented all that was good in the previous cycle. She was the embodiment of the reward of their labour. Many mythological accounts give earth itself as the embodiment of Goddess Lakshmi, who is variously known as Dharani, Sri or Kamala. She is what you aspire for. Shree means prosperity or glory, the reward of riches. She is the symbolic representation of any achievement. She also means earth with all its resources. It was the earth itself which was retrieved from that catastrophe known as Pralaya. That she married Vishnu is a natural corollary of the thought process which made Vishnu the preserver of the earth. Taking recourse to modern analogy we can say that if Vishnu is the General Manager of the Creation, Lakshmi represents the resources that the Manager has at his command. In this sense Lakshmi is not a character but just a concept. She is said to be the Goddess of all riches and prosperity. Implied by this means that all those who have their desires fulfilled have the grace of Lakshmi. In the colloquial parlance, when a person falls on evil days, it is said that "Lakshmi has become angry with that fellow." Lakshmi's grace ensures all comforts and facilities. She is not only the Goddess of riches and prosperity, she is the ultimate reward of any endeavour. That she is Vishnu's espouse means that if one manages his affairs well one shall always get the reward. She is bracketed with Vishnu because of a logical argument of the ancient Hindu brain.

The Hindu belief holds three functions mainly responsible in the process of creation : creation, preservation and destruction and the three Super Gods of the Hindu Trinity : Brahma, Vishnu and Mahesh (Shiv) are the incharge of these functions. Purely from the modern view we can say that he who is responsible for creation must have the facility of wisdom or intelligence, and hence the association of Saraswati with Brahma; who is responsible for preservation must have full resources and funds at his command, and hence the association of Lakshmi with Vishnu; who is responsible for destruction must have the effective destroying power, hence the association of Goddess Kali, Durga or Chandi with Lord Shiv. Not that they were chosen by any one; these pairs developed over a very long period in the logic of the ancient brain. Obviously their logic still appears quite reasonable. So Vishnu was the ideal choice for Lakshmi and she married him.

Lakshmi was not only considered Goddess of riches but also of beauty in many mythological renderings "It is quite likely that, because of the underlying human desire for wealth and beauty, she absorbed a large number of folk elements during her evolution into a widely accepted member of the pantheon"—so opines A.G. Mitchell the famous indologist. Lakshmi is depicted as the embodiment of all the aspirations of a peace loving man; wealth, riches, prosperity, in contradiction to the depiction of Durga or Kali when these qualities are not stressed but her ferocity is highlighted. This is what it appears now but in the ancient stages when the concept of the goddess was being developed, all female deities were believed to be repository of all chivalry and ferocity. The hymn sung by Indra, the gods's chief describes Lakshmi also as 'Mahāraudraroopini', meaning having terrible appearance. As a matter of fact the images of the gods and goddesses keep on changing with time. The ancient brain, having chosen his deities and established their efficacy, began to classify in two distinct categories: male and female. Since nothing in the universe is unisexual how could the gods be deprived of this process?

So their female form also began to be developed which was later on associated with its Male counterpart of the divine existence. According to Mitchell, "As Hinduism developed, the status of female deities slowly changed from that of mother, sister or daughter to the representation of the single abstract idea of the sole principle of creative energy. Later, this principle was envisaged as being the active power of the impersonal absolute (Brahman), who was too remote to undertake executive responsibilities and therefore not able to respond to prayers. Eventually this active power was personified in the form of the goddess Devi who could not only respond but also satisfy the worshippers' desire for someone whom devotion (Bhakti) could be directed : Further religious developments resulted (by about 5th century A.D.) in Devi manifesting herself in many different forms as the active power of male deities or as deified symbols of abstract ideas associated with them as Triple-knowledge (Trayi-Vidya), Fierce (Chandi), and Revered (Arya). In the group opposite, Shridevi represents wealth (Lakshmi) and Bhudevi (also called Prithvi) the Earth. Eventually this active principle of male deities was formalised as their 'shakti' which enables the pantheon conveniently to be extended and gave the worshipper the choice of approaching the deity directly, indirectly through his 'shakti' or of invoking the 'shakti' itself".

Lakshmi, since being associated with wealth, prosperity and land (as Bhudevi), came to be associated with agriculture produce as well. In Sanskrit to be 'dhan-dhanya poorna' means having wealth and edible things in ample quantities. 'Dhan' is the term for money which also forms the root for Dhaan or Dhaanya which means agricultural wealth. In those hoary times the basic concept of prosperity was limited to having ample cereals. Since agriculture was the financial base of the society, Lakshmi came to be associated with agricultural produce also. Mitchell says: .."(Lakshmi) as Sitā (wife of Rām) she was said to have been born from a furrow. This has obvious links with agriculture, and its imagery is immediately apparent when it is associated with the working of the Indian plough. The symbolism is again emphasised when she is called Earth (Dharani) as the wife of Vishnu when he was Rāma with the Axe (Parashuram)."

Lakshmi's One name is also 'Ramaa', which means she who roams about everywhere. 'Ramana' also means to be lost in, engrossed, immersed or absorbed. It is said that once Lord Vishnu was resting in his abode Vaikuntha when the sage Revat reached there riding his stallion, Uchhaishravaa. Goddess Lakshmi, who was also present with her Lord was so enchanted by the beauty of that horse that she lost awareness of everything else. Even when Lord Vishnu called her and shook her by her hand she failed to emerge from her reverie. Vishnu lost temper at the open defiance of his command by his spouse and cursed her that henceforth she would be known as 'Ramaa' (or the one who ever roams about), who would by nature be fickle and unreliable.[1] If we take the term Ramaa's 'roaming about' meaning, her fickleness becomes self-evident. This name of Lakshmi suits well with a name or ephithet of her spouse's own form Rām' (Raam) which means 'he with whom is instinct everything of the world'. But if we take the other meaning of the term 'Ramaa' it would mean that she is or her attributes are engrossing for everyone. Obviously! Who does not want money or prosperity?

Lakshmi's association or link with the Earth has already been hinted at. Some scholars opine that initially when land was the only possession worth the name, Lakshmi and Bhudevi were one. Later on when gold, jewellery and other riches appeared more precious for the ancients they distinguished Lakshmi from Bhudevi. That Bhudevi was the original concept of the Goddess is apparent from the Vedas also. The Harrappan flat stone discs show nude female forms who probably represent the Mother Earth or Bhudevi. There is also a group of scholars who regard that Shakambhari (the goddess of vegetation) was originally conceived as the Mother Earth. The name of the goddess is

---

1. The whole story is given in the next chapter.

connected with the agriculture and plantation during the Aryan and post-Aryan period. It appears when the worshippers of the fertility aspect of female deity came into prominence, the process of distinguishing Lakshmi from Bhudevi began. Then the distinction was made between the goddesses with positive aspects and the goddesses with the negative aspects. Both Lakshmi and Saraswati belong to the first category.

Although Lakshmi is adored by all, with the classification of the society into four categories by Manu, she became the chosen deity of the traders and business men. Hence her special worship at Deepavali which is a special festival of this class. Many a legend avers that the goddess Lakshmi emerged from the ocean on this very day. This could be true but cause of special worship of Lakshmi at Deepāvali is much more deeper than its this simple explanation.

As mentioned earlier, whole of the episode of the churning of ocean is an allegory. It symbolically represents the effort of the people setting their house in order after the onslaught of rains. Initially living conditions were not as they were later on and rains used to be nothing short of Pralaya. The ancients regarded scorching summers to autumn as the period of Pralaya when first heat and then water troubled then greatly. These four months (roughly from June to Sept.) were regarded as the period of stay for even the roving Mahatmas and ascetics and the practice is still maintaned by the devout. According to the Indian school of astronomy, 'Shukra' or Venus 'sinks' down the horizon and this indicates cessation of all auspicious ceremonies for these four months, especially in north India. The ceremonies start again on Devuthan Ekadashi (the 11th bright day of the months of Kartik, i.e. around 1st week of November). This cessation of all festivities is, actually, more caused by the climatic conditions and less by any astrological considerations. In India, even about a couple of hundred years back, braving the natural onslaughts of heat and rains was certainly an onerous task. Moreover, in villages it was really a problem to celebrate anything important during this phase of total lull. Hence the cessation of the festivities. It is only after the rains that people come out of their 'hibernation' and take the view of the world afresh. In north India specially, the devout begin their activities by first remembering the dead and performing the 'Shraadha'. Then they look at Nature after its face has been washed by rains. They find the earth emitting a pleasant fragrance so they start their worship with devotion to the Mother Goddess—call it the Mother Earth or Durga or whatever. They remember Durga more in the gesture of thanksgiving as they could survive the terrible season when all the negative factors—the demons—disturbed them most, by the Goddess's grace. Having assessed their strength, the kings used to start their victory expeditions on the Tenth Day of the bright half of Ashwin (Oct-beginning) now known as Dusshera or Vijayadashmi. It was only around Diwali that their armies used to return to the capital with their loot and other rewards. The soldiers used to settle their account with the grocers etc. around that time. So, Diwali became the most auspicious day for the traders and the business class. That custom is still pervalent. It is customary to worship the account books and other financial records. Basically this function was of the traders class or the businessmen whose chosen deity is Lakshmi, the goddess of prosperity. The Goddess is worshipped on this occasion with Ganesh. Ganesh's worship has assumed importance owing to this deity's infinite capacity to create and remove hurdles. He is the Vighneshwar, the lord of all impediments. So on this day Lakshmi is worshipped for wealth and prosperity while Ganesh is worshipped for getting that prosperity unhindered. In conformity with the olden concept which regarded Lakshmi as the goddess of the agricultural produce also, the freshly produced corn or rice are offered to the twin deities.

Lighting lamps on Deepavali night has an astronomical cum psychological reason. According to the Indian astrology the sun becomes weakest when it comes in the Libra or Tula sign or rashi. That is the sun's debilitation sign. In the month when the

Sun is in its debilitation sign and the moon is absent (being the moonless night) comes the darkest Amavasya. That is supposed to be the darkest hour when out of the two luminaries, the sun goes in its debilitation and the moon is altogether absent. Obviously it must be having the psychological effect. In order to ward off that darkest hour and boost up their morale, the ancients devised a novel method : lighting lamps to fight that darkest hour and blasting crackers to ward off the potential danger from the beasts and evil spirits. That custom is still followed with great enthusiasm.

Another significant feature of this Deepavali festivity is gambling. Since many a part of the country reckons this day as the first day of the new year, the people wish to test their luck through gambling on this occasion. Whole night gambling session after the "Lakshmi Poojan" is a regular feature of this night of Celebration. Why do they test their luck this way has also a very revealing explanation. It is said in our scriptures that "Lakshmi comes through Adharma (immoral practices) stays with Dharma but goes away again through Adharma". This again has a psycho-socio basis.

The ancient Indian mind, rooted in the concept that all material wealth and riches are ephemeral and fey, never agreed to one's getting immense wealth with moralistic efforts. One may get the reward of one's labour but not immeasurable wealth. Accumulation of wealth ever appeared to have a sinister aura round it. That 'Sone-Ki Lanka' could be a hide-out of all that was vile was a foregone conclusion for the devout Hindu. Although gold has remained a dearest metal for the entire human race—its Sanskrit term 'Suvarna' literally means 'the best colour' or hue— the inherent evil connotations always seem to envelop this metal. All the stories about the recovery of a lost treasure— buried in deep caves or trenches—have snakes or serpents—the symbol of evil—invariable covering it. This inherent thought of association of evil with gold or riches convinced the ancient mind that one comes into massive affluence only by one's association with evil. Hence Lakshmi's coming to grace one's life through Adharma. The concept is still held valid and no one who comes into riches escape being bracketed with something illegal and immoral. It is not uncommon to see people casting sarcastic remarks on seeing the flamboyant display of wealth: "the black-money has to show itself" or "no one with honest means can have this much of wealth." If one reads even the oldest mythological stories or literary or even folk stories, association of evil with riches figures perennially.

The second aspect of wealth or Lakshmi is heir stay at a particular place. The scriptures say that she stays with Dharma; that is, she stays when one leads a pious life, devoid of any immoral activities. That belief is also accepted even till to-day. We find most of the charitable institutions, temples etc., invariably constructed by rich men, big business tycoons and industrialists. These persons blessed with the grace of goddess Lakshmi believe that doing work for the religious or noble cause would absolve them from all sins they might have accrued in getting the blessing of the goddess of riches. This could be their attempt to launder away the stigma attached to their being rich—the stigma of the evil association. Even the Gandhian concept of "Trusteeship" highlights this very fact. Gandhiji was, unlike the communists, not against the rich. He always maintained that this class is as necessary to a society as food to man, for it knows how to earn money. This could be another moot issue: how they did it. But they know the art of minting money. But, according to Gandhi ji, they must apportion a part of their wealth for the general welfare of society. There is no conflict in the Gandhian thought between the haves and have-nots. He strongly advocated that the 'haves' must care for the 'have-nots' voluntarily in order to earn the social merit. He showed the path of synthesis in his unique way.

As a matter of fact, this Gandhian thought is a natural corollary to the basic concept that Lakshmi stays with Dharma. It says that having collected wealth by whatever means possible, one should endeavour to preserve it by being good to others. Hence we see in every big company or organisation, various accounts or the 'Dharmadhas' are reserved for the charitable purposes. One may say that these activities are the process of atonement one undergoes to maintain one's riches. The goddess Lakshmi is fickle by nature and he who takes extra care to fulfil her taxing demands manages to have her longer association. The brilliant, original thinker of ancient India, Chanakya, also says that :

'Chalā Lakshmishchalah prānāshchale jeevit- mandire
Chalāchale cha sansāre Dharm eko hi nishchalah |

[Everything in the world is fickle and fey: be it Lakshmi (Prosperity), life, body—anything! What is everlasting is Dharma only].

Thus if the fickle stays, with the stable, naturally the stay of the fickle would also be longer.

The third concept that Lakshmi goes away with Adharma is a universal fact. Each race has its idioms highlighting this very fact. The English saying "ill-gotten ill spent" also emphasises the same fact. In this context a very popular ritual performed at Deepavali is worth elaborating.

That popular ritual in gambling, about which a passing reference has already been given. Gambling for the entire night and keeping the lighted lamps specially near the gutter-exists or exhausts in the houses have identical reason. The exhaust holes or the 'Morees' symbolise the wrong way of entry into the house. Since it is said that surest way of Lakshmi's entry into one's house is through the wrong or unfair way, the custom gained prevalence that one should keep the exhaust holes also well-lit to welcome the goddess. However, there is also a scientific necessity to observe this ritual. Normally the traditional Hindu houses give least importance to public hygiene in contradistinction to the great emphasis laid on personal hygiene. There might be devout Hindus having bath twice or thrice daily even during the biting winters, but rarely one would find their even kitchen-exhaust or the 'Rasoi ki Nali' clean, let alone the bathroom's exhaust. And these exhausts are the places the insects and bugs etc., breed most. Thus cleaning these exhaust even once a year is a very welcome ritual. The age-old practice of the Hindu tenets—to mix scientific requirements with religious dictates—is quite apparent in this practice. Thus cleaning the outlets for welcoming Lakshmi and keeping the lighted lamps burning for the convenience of the goddess is a very healthy practice, notwithstanding the wrong reason—that Lakshmi comes into one's house by the wrong way—attributed to it. This wrong reason also goes to explain people's gambling for the entire Deepavali night or for many nights preceding and following this Darkest Night. It is they who invite Lakshmi to come the wrong way, little realising that for this goddess's entry and exit have similar gates. If she comes by the wrong way, she also leaves the same way. But unmindful of the negative possibility, people still indulge in gambling as though they are performing some holy act ordained by the scriptures. They must realise that Lakshmi comes in and goes out the same immoral way.

Lakshmi has been depicted as being the chosen deity of the Vaishya-category; an object of respectable enjoyment for the Kshtriyas, and a positive anathema to Brahmans. This statement is quite self evident in the first case which has been discussed at length. In the second case her position is also self-explanatory because for the kings (or the modern tycoons of industry) money is what it does. Earning money is not the sole aim of the Kshatriyas or the Administrators but earning power and reputation in which Lakshmi provides only a means and not the end.

The valiants in ancient times cared more for their power and might and this goddess was just a tool to make them achieve their end. Money was needed by them for raising huge armies and fighting wars to aggrandise their empires or kingdoms. Thus she was an object of 'Bhog' or 'useful enjoyment' for the Kshatriyas. So, she was the aim for the traders and means for Kshatriyas. But what is or was her status in the eyes of the Brahmans? In this context a shloka from 'Chanakyaneeti' is aptly quotable. In that shloka, the Goddess Lakshmi expressed her anger for the Brahmans. She says :

"Peetah kruddhena tātashcharana tala hato vallabhoyen roshā

Aabalya dwi-pravaryeih swavadanavivare dhāryate vairireme

Gehans me chhedayanti pratidivasasamakanta poojanimittat

Tasmāt khinna sadaaham dwijakulanilayam nāth yuktam tyajami |"

"He who drank up my father, the ocean, in his anger (was a brahman). He who kicked my husband in the bosom (was a brahman). They who place upon their tongue my arch enemy (are also brahmans). They who pluck away my lotus for the worship of Shiv (are also brahmans). These brahmans have ruined my life. Now I would never spare their house with my wrath."

The first reference is of the sage Agastya who drank the entire ocean in his rage, the second one is of the sage Bhrigu who kicked Vishnu in the bosom; the third is for the Goddess Saraswati and the fourth one is the general reference for all the brahmans. Goddess Lakshmi expresses her anger against brahmans with quite an emphasis.

Although this observation of Chanakya has its mythological relevance, through this Shloka Chanakya has indirectly proved the brahmans' contempt for Lakshmi. Since a brahman is supposed to be that highly intelligent and spiritually mighty person whoever lives in communion with eternity, why should he care for a goddess who can bestow only material riches and prosperity. For him these worldly benefits are of no use. Hence his contempt for Lakshmi.

But if we analyse the fact with little more attention, we would realise that cause of material adversity among the brahmans is not due to any lack of resources but owing to lack of the will. All through the Hindu belief has been advocating against material possessions—right from the Geeta to present day literary creations. This belief says that these materials give rise to desire, which leads to infatuation and hence, eventually to ignorance. Thus he who wishes to remain untainted by and aloof from the lucre of the body must show indifference if not contempt to such a goddess whose area of influence does not go beyond the world and body. Hence Goddess Lakshmi's indifference to brahmans or to those pay scant attention to material riches.

Goddess Lakshmi is said to be fickle because she wants full attention to keep her in one's control. A little carelessness can drive her out. Again, a quotation from 'Chanakyaneeti' puts this fact rather succinctly.

"Kuchailinam dantmalopadharinam
  Bahvaashinam nishthurbhāshitam cha |
 Suryodaye chāstmite shyānām
  Vimunchite shreeyardi Chakrapānih ||"

Meaning, he who wears dirty clothes; whose teeth are full of filth; who eats like a glutton; who utters harsh speech; who sleeps for the entire day (from the sunrise to sun set)—Lakshmi deserts such a person even if that person be Lord Vishnu (the Chakra Weilder) himself.

What Chanakya emphasises through his this maxim is that if one is careless one may not get the blessings of Goddess Lakshmi. One should be careful in what one eats, how one sleeps, how one behaves with others etc. In short you can't afford too be callous and indifferent in your behaviour if you want to stay rich. That way the Goddess makes very taxing demand on her devotees. No wonder all those who are really rich and wish to remain so have to follow a very strict regimen. And that is why the rich persons suffer a variety of ailments caused by their over-taxing their body and mind to keep the Goddess within their homes.

But keeping your money unused is also a sure sign of your inviting adversity. You must know to how to rotate your money profitably. You just cannot keep this fickle (chanchala) dame captive. She must get enough room for movement. In other words, one must know how to spend or invest this money. In one of his maxims Chanakya, the most practical thinker among the ancients, says that if Lakshmi is kept bound within the confines of a house like the daughter-in-law of a prestigious family, she becomes useless and sick. But she also becomes useless and cheap if like a prostitute she becomes available for all and sundry. In other words, money is what it does. Hence accumulating money should not be the aim, it is to be used judiciously if you want to be prosperous. As Bacon said centuries ago "Money is a good servant but a bad master." Those who are moneyed know how to use it. Lakshmi despite being a 'Chanchala' (fast moving, fickle) stays for ever with Vishnu because he treats her as his wife and not as his mother! Lakshmi stays with Vishnu because he is a clean god, clad in fine clothes and looks charming. That is the reason of Lakshmi's falling instantly for Vishnu and not even casting a side glance towards Shiv who is indifferent to his appearance and careless in his behaviour. Those who aspire to get blessing of this goddess must have a beautious form also, besides a willing spirit.

Although Garuda is also described to be the mount of Goddess Lakshmi, her traditonally accepted vehicle is an owl. Now, owl or 'Ulooka' in Sanskrit, is a bird, which is described to be a dullard in Indian parlance but according to the western belief it is a very cunning bird. It has the special quality of seeing through the darkness. It is generally held that this bird sleeps through the day and prowls through the might. It is said that owing to its lethargic and dull nature the Goddess takes it for a ride! She is handmaiden of those who know how to control it; how to make best use of her resources like Lord Vishnu. But those who blindly worship her are verily the owls or 'Ulookas'. The choice is ours: whether we wish to be Lord Vishnu or the 'Ulooka' in our association with Lakshmi.

3. Goddess Lakshmi: In Various Mythological Legends

(i) Goddess Lakshmi's Incarnation as Tulsi (Basil Plant)

Long long ago the descendent of Daksha Prajapati, Kushadhvaj performed a severe penance to get Lakshmi as his daughter. At last the Goddess was pleased to fulfil his desire and took birth as his daughter. Since the girl was able to recite the pious Vedic Incantations right at the time of her birth, she was given 'Vedavati' name. She was a very devoted girl to Lord Vishnu right since her childhood. As she grew she began to perform great penance to get the Lord as her husband.

Once when she was performing worship in the quietness of a jungle, Ravan reached there in the form of an eremite guest. As was the custom followed by the hermits doing penance in jungles, she welcomed the guest, offering flowers and fruits. While she was looking after the comforts of the guest, the guest, Ravan, was enchanted by her fair beauty and wanted to make love. The girl resisted but when she found Ravan's amorous advances quite overpowering, she cursed Ravan "Since you are trying to overpower a weak and unprotected woman (girl), I curse you that your end shall be caused by a woman only." So saying she immolated herself by jumping into a pit having the burning fire. It was Vedavati who, in one of the coming births appeared as Sita to cause Ravan's death and downfall.

In her next birth she appeared as the daughter of King Dharmadhwaj and his wife Madhavi. This beautiful daughter was called Tulsi. Owing to her previous birth's memories, she was very much devoted to Lord Vishnu. Getting instructions from the sage Narad she began to perform very severe austerities to get Lord Vishnu as her husband. But by Narad's advice she first sought the blessings of Lord Brahma. The deity appeared before her and knowing about her intention, declared: "Dear girl!

Owing to the curse of Shree Rādhā ji, Sudāmā the Gop (cowman), born of Lord Krishna's partial grace, has appeared in this life as King Shankhachooda. In your one of the lives you both were quite enamoured of each other but could not meet due to the social taboos. In order to get rid of that unfulfilled passionate desire and be pious again, in this life you are first destined to marry Shankhachooda. Then after the Goddess Saraswati would curse you for some of your lapse to become a tree. Only then you would get Nārāyan as your spouse."

Getting that message from Brahma, Tulsi began to wait for that auspicious day when she was destined to meet Lord Vishnu. But as was destined, one day, while she was still in the jungle, she happened to meet the king Shankhachooda. Looking at each other in those comely surroundings both were instantly drawn to each other. Lord Brahma immediately appeared there and having introduced both of them to each other, tied the nuptial knot with full Vedic ritual. Then Tulsi went with Shankhachooda and began to dwell happily in her husband's capital. Owing to her very fortunate wife, his strength began to grow leaps and bounds. In no time he converted his small kingdom into a big empire. Soon his empire began to threaten the independent status of the gods, demons, the Gandharvas, the Kinnar and every other race. All of them immediately rushed to Lords Brahma and Shiv who advised them to meet Lord Vishnu, their celebrated troubleshooter. Lord Vishnu, when they approached him, heard them patiently and devised a plan for their redemption from the trouble.

According to the plan of Lord Vishnu, Lord Shankar sent Pushpadanta as messenger to Shankhachood to warn him to remain within his limits. But when this warning had no deterrent effect on Chandrachooda who continued to make advances in the divine territory, Lord Shiv ordered his army to get ready for launching the assault and his henchmen led by Skanda and supported by Veerbhadra with his dreadful troops of goblins and haunds began to await eagerly the confrontation.

Meanwhile Shankhachood was somewhat scared by the divine threat. So one day he disclosed all that transpired between him and the gods. "I am really scared as to what they are upto. They can ruin me."

"Nothing of the sort will happen till I am around. I have great faith in my protective powers which I developed by being a fully devoted and faithful wife. Nothing untoward can happen to the husband whose wife is faithful and honest. Shed off your worries. Come let us enjoy life as much as we can." And saying so, Tulsi took Chandrachood to their bed chamber.

Next morning when he heard that the divine army, led by Shiv, was at his border, Chandrachood also readied his army and reached undaunted to take on the divine forces. His wife's confidence had also fortified his spiritis. Soon both the armies were engaged in a fierce battle which continued for even hundred years indecisively. The gods were rather perplexed to witness king Chandrachooda's incomparable valour. He looked invincible. Even Lord Shiv, Skand etc., could not defeat him. When the gods saw Chandrachooda's incomparable valour they again rushed to Lord Vishnu, who advised them : "Don't be worried, O gods! This Chandrachood is deriving his illimitable power from his wife's chaste behaviour."

Then Shiv opined : "Is there no way by which his wife's devotion to her husband be disturbed? This has to be done otherwise this demon lord would disturb the divine authority in the world. Lord, you must do something."

Realising that the moment of reckoning was about to come concerning his meeting and fulfilling the desire of Tulsi, Lord Vishnu assured them that he would soon play a trick upon the tyrant demon.

Next day, when the war was being raged with great ferocity, Chandrachooda found an old brahman appearing before him, and asking for a desired boon to be fulfilled. In the heat of the battle, he said : "Tathāstu!" (So be it), without even knowing whatever that oldman was desiring.

That old man was none else but Lord Vishnu in disguise. Getting the boon he straightaway repaired to the orchard. Tulsi was busy in her worship. Tulsi was surprised to see her husband appearing there alone, with no trace upon his visage of the tension due to the conflict with the divinities. Soon she heard the sound of blowing horns and conches heralding victory. Upon enquiry she learnt that the gods' army reconciled to the fact of Chandrachooda's supremacy and retreated. This was a great news to Tulsi who rejoiced greatly and fell in the open arms of her husband. But he whom she thought to be her husband was actually Lord Vishnu in the disguise of Chandrachooda. As she fell in the arms of 'her husband' her wifely devotion was vitiated. That very moment Chandrachood, still engaged in the battle with Lord Shiv's army felt ineffably weak and in no time Lord Shiv's trident beheaded him.

As soon as Tulsi, the incarnate form of Lakshmi, learnt about the deceit Lord Vishnu had played on her, she got a terrible shock. She cursed Vishnu "O Lord! How could you be so stone-hearted as to deceive me so cunningly. Now I curse you that in the coming epoch you would also suffer a great disturbance due to your wife's abduction by a demon."

Then Vishnu clarified his position : "O Devi! I am none else but Vishnu whose wife you ever wished to be. It is to fulfil that order of the providence that I had to act foul with you. Now I shall ever remain with you."

"I am blessed to get you, O Lord," replied Tulsi or Vrinda, but added: "Since you wilfully tried to pollute my chastity, hardening your heart for the gods' victory, I curse you to become a stone." And soon she herself was petrified to being a small tree (plant) of basil and the Lord, in order to fulfil the curse the pious lady had charged him with, became a tiny piece of stone, known as Shaligram[1] which ever remains near the basil plant. Lord Brahma immediately appeared there to solemnise their marriage and ever since the two remain together.

Thus Lakshmi, in the form of Vrinda or Tulsi came to incarnate herself in the form of plant and Lord Vishnu in the form of a stone. They have remained together ever since.

(ii) Goddess Lakshmi's Incarnation as a Mare

Once Lord Vishnu was merrily resting in his abode, Vaikunth, when astride his divine stallion 'Uchchaishrava' arrived sage Raivat. Goddess Lakshmi was also with her Lord. Seeing that extra-ordinary horse the Goddess was so much enchanted that she became indifferent to everything else and kept on staring at the horse. She was so deeply lost in her reverie that even when Lord Vishnu shook her physically by holding her arm, she remained indifferent to him. Seeing her espouse defying his commands, the Lord grew angry and he cursed his own spouse. "Since you showed indifference to me and the sage by remaining lost in your reverie, I curse you that henceforth you shall be called 'Ramaa' owing to your fickle nature and you shall be reliable to no body. You shall ever be roaming about the world in the form of a mare."

This curse jerked the Goddess out of her reverie and she was very sad for her lapse. Then she entreated her Lord to forgive her and promised that henceforth she would ever remain devoted to him only. The Lord relented somewhat at Lakshmi's entreaty and modified his curse by saying that she would return to Vaikunth after producing a colt in her mare form.

According to the curse pronounced, Lakshmi came to the confluence of the rivers Yamuna and Tamasa in the mare form and began to devote her time in worshipping Lord Shiv. Pleased

---

[1]. It is sacred dark grey coloured stone worshipped by the Vaishnavites and supposed to be pervaded by the presence of Vishnu. Chemically it is stone containing fossil ammonite. Shaligram is believed to be Lord Vishnu's symbol as phallus or Lingam is Lord Shiv's symbol.

by the mare's (Laskshmi's) devout worship, Lord Shiv appeared there with his consort Uma and said: "O Goddess! Don't worry. Your accursed days are likely to end soon. Remember that there is no difference between me and Lord Vishnu. We are the manifestation of the same Supreme Spirit."

"I know this, great Lord!", replied the mare (Lakshmi) and added: "Once my Lord had also told me this very fact." Then narrating the whole episode concerning her taking the mare form by her Lord's curse, she requested early redemption from her distress. Whereupon Lord Shiv told her that soon Lord Vishnu would appear on the earth in the form of a horse and he would produce a male issue by his contact with her. Then she would return to her Lord's realm, Vaikunth.

Reassuring her this way, Lord Shiv, returned to his abode, Kailash Mount, and when the time was due, he asked his one of the hench men, Chitraroop to go to Vishnu and request him to appear on the earth as a horse. Getting the message, Vishnu did so. While roaming on the earth, he (the horse) happened to meet a comely mare on the bank of the river Yumuna. As was willed by Destiny he made physical contact with that mare (Lakshmi) and in due time the mare produced a beautiful colt. As she produced the colt, Lakshmi's period of the curse expired and she returned to Vaikunth. Lord Vishnu also followed suit leaving that colt in the care of the Gandharva Turvasu. That colt was almost like a boy with horse like features and he became the progenitor of the dynasty called 'Haihaya vansha' after his own name Haihaya.

(iii) Goddess Lakshmi's Role in Demon Jalandhar's Episode

Long-long ago, one day the gods' chief Indra and the divine priest Brihaspati went to Kailash mount to have Lord Shankar's Darshan. In order to test their intelligence Lord Shankar disguised himself as a bearded hermit and sat before the mount. Reaching near when Indra asked the hermit about the Lord, the former kept silent. Drunk in the wine of his exalted position, Indra felt insulted by the hermit's behaviour and tried to hit the hermit with his thunderbolt. But owing to the grace of the Lord, the thunderbolt lost its sharpness and the blow proved innocuous. But it was enough to incite Lord Shankar's wrath. His eyes began to emit fire of his anger. Seeing that dreadful fire, the divine priest immediately recognised Lord Shankar and requested him to pardon Indra's ignorance. Though he acceded to Brihaspati's request, the fire from his third eye in the forehead could not be doused. At last Lord Shankar took that fire in his hand and threw it in the Ocean of Milk. Just after a moment that beacon of fire was transformed into a robust boy who began to cry loudly, disturbing all the protectors of the directions (Digpals). On their request Brahma ji went near the boy. When Brahma ji took that boy in his hands that grisly boy, pressed the Creators's neck so powerfully by his hands that Brahma ji had tears welling up his eyes in that unbearable agony. Seeing the fate of that robust boy Brahma predicted that boy was going to become a mighty demon king. He also gave him 'Jalandhar' name. He also made the forecast that no one except Lord Shiv would be able to slay that demon and that this demon's wife would be very beautiful and very faithful to him.

The ocean reared the boy up and when he came of age, he got him married to Vrinda, the daughter of the demon called Kalinemi. Shukrācharya, the demon priest, was quite impressed with the immense power of Jalandhar and he appointed him as the king of the demons.

Once while he was holding his court, the demon priest reached there. During the course of the discussion Jalandhar learnt how Vishnu had cheated the gods by gifting away to the gods all the precious gems churned out of the ocean. Hearing this Jalandhar blew up and there and then he sent a messenger with the ultimatum that either the gods returned the precious gems or faced the war. The gods accepted the challenge and a fierce war broke out between the gods and the demons. Owing to the "Sanjeevani Vidya" (the science of reviving the dead) the demon priest knew, he was able to bring dead demons back to life. But when Jalandhar saw that gods were not dying he was baffled and asked the demon priests its reason "O priest", asked the demon,"how could the gods be revived when you alone know the Sanjeevani vidya?" "Their priest, Brihaspati knows about a special herb growing on the Dronagiri. That is equally effective to revive the dead. If you could have that hill thrown into the sea, may be, you can defeat them."

Jalandhar immediately went on to the Himalayas and uprooting the hill with his bare hands, threw it down the sea. Since the gods' supply of life-reviving herb dwindled they began to lose. At last Jalandhar captured their capital Amaravati and the gods were thrown away. Defeated and distressed they took shelter in the caves of the Himalayas and Indra again started to summon his disarrayed forces to take on the demons. Having regrouped his army, Indra sought Lord Vishnu's counsel about his future course of action.

Now Lord Vishnu was in a great fix. His beloved spouse Lakshmi, upon knowing that the demon Jalandhar was also a product of the ocean and hence her brother, had forced him to his committing about not slaying the demon who was like a brother-in-law to him. When Indra sought his advice, he was somewhat non-plussed about his own course of action. Then he resolved that he would fight with the gods against the demon but would not make any attempt to kill him.

The gods then again launched a massive attack on the demons. Lord Vishnu was directing the divine army from the rear. But the demons fought so bravely that Indra had to beat a hasty retreat. Then Vishnu came to the front riding his favourite mount, Garuda. Jalandhar faced Vishnu with equal ferocity, covering his entire body by raining his innumerable keen arrows. Then Vishnu summoned his favourite weapon, Chakra Sudarshan, and hacked off all the arrows surrounding him. Then both began to fight with redoubled vigour. Jalandhar fought so fearlessly and so bravely that Vishnu was pleased with his martial prowess and during the battle, asked the demon to seek his boon from him. But this time Jalandhar had also learnt about his relationship with Lakshmi from his priest and said : " O Lord! You are my brother-in-law and even otherwise quite adorable. I request you to cease fighting and accept my invitation of passing some days happily in my kingdom with your spouse and my sister Lakshmi." Smilingly Vishnu replied : "So be it!"And after sometime he left, along with his spouse Lakshmi and reached Jalandhar's capital. Jalandhar was greatly obliged and looked after his sister and brother-in-laws' all comforts. Lord Vishnu's this visit subdued his enemies automatically and he began to rule happily with great piety and justice. He had become so pious and sobre due to Lord Vishnu's association that he began to worship all the Supergods of the Trinity with special leaning towards Lord Shiv whom he found, by the past references quite impartial to gods and demons and who treated them alike.

The gods were aghast to find their own leader so tactfully won over by their arch enemy. They tried their best but owing to Goddess Lakshmi's influence, Lord Vishnu could not be approached. At last, frustrated in their attempt the gods went to Kailash and told Shiv about their plight. Although Shiv himself was willing to help the gods, he found no chink in Jalandhar's armour to declare his hostility. The effect of Jalandhar's devout worship was also reaching near him and he was also gradually getting propitiated. Jalandhar had created such pitiable condition of the gods that they felt totally shelterless and weak. So, they together worshipped Lord Shankar and requested him. But they could not make Shankar fight Jalandhar.

Then they sought the help of the sage Narad who was past master in creating dissension even between two friends. Narad heard their sorry tale and reassured them that soon he would do something to turn Shankar hostile to Jalandhar.

One day while Jalandhar was sitting in his court, the sage Narad, to whom no place in the universe was inaccessible owing to his receiving a special boon from Lord Vishnu, reached there. Jalandhar welcomed him very reverentially by washing his feet and offering choicest food. Then he asked the sage: "O Great Sage! What made you come to my capital? If you are here just for the heck of it, I am honoured. But if you feel I need your advice and that is the reason of your coming here, please tell me without any hesitation. If you need anything, just mention it and it will be before you!"

Narad replied: "I don't need any thing, O King! I had heard a great praise about your kingdom so I came here. You really have everything. Your coffers are full, your wife is very faithful and your people are very loyal. I came to see whether all that I had heard about your kingdom is true or not."

"Do you find my kingdom lacking in anything sage?" asked Jalandhar rather haughtily. That was the moment Narad was waiting for. The moment anyone starts behaving haughtily, the evil forces possess one which invariably confuse one's mind.

"No, you don't lack anything," Narad began in quite a diplomatic way. "But a king's glory is not judged by his valiant troops and riches only. The ancients believed that the number of beautiful women a king possesses makes him rise in stature. You have much less beautiful ladies, let alone of any outstanding beauty. You should have some outstanding beautiful women in your kingdom. This is the only thing you lack."

"But how to get that lady," Jalandhar asked, "for all those I know of are in my harem already."

"No", Narad said emphatically, "There is one most beautiful I have ever seen. She is in the possession of Lord Shiv. Her name is Parvati. In fact, I am coming from Shiv's realm only."

Hearing this Jalandhar immediately sent his messenger to Kailash with the express desire that Parvati should be sent to his realm. His this remark was enough to incite Lord Shankar's wrath. When Shiv refused the demon came to attack him. Narad had polluted his brain so totally that he did not mind attacking the very Lord he had been worshiping all this while. After a long battle the demon was beheaded by Shiv's trident. Since the demon was deriving his power from his wife's chaste and loyal attitude, Shiv had managed to make Vishnu ruin her chastity.[2] Only then that demon, the scourge of the gods, could be killed.

Then enlightening the gods after their victory, Lord Shiv said : "It is difficult to get away from infatuation which leads to confusion and ruin. Even Lord Vishnu was duped by it. Infatuated to his wife Lakshmi, he began to side with the demons, leaving the gods in the lurch."

"But Lord", Indra asked "I have never heard or seen Lord Vishnu getting infatuated to anyone earlier. How he suffered it this time?"

"He suffered because", Lord Shiv said, "in the fit of his rage he even cursed Lakshmi to become a mare only because she happened to be indifferent, for a few moments, to him. Whenever any one loses one's balance and sense of propriety that one gets infatuated."

At that time Lord Vishnu also reached there and said : "Lord Shiv has said it very rightly. I suffered the loss of balance and hence infatuation. When even I can become victim of this lapse, no wonder you all and humans also suffer it repeatedly. In one of my coming Incarnations, I shall tell the world how to cure this frailty of mind."

Lord Vishnu did so in his Incarnation as Lord Krishna by giving the message through his 'Geeta.'

---

2. For more details read "Lord Shiv" of the same series.

(iv) Goddess Lakshmi's Worship by Indra

Once the chief of gods, Indra was indulging in amorous dalliance in the company of the Apsara (divine danseuse) Rambha in the quietness of a shaded jungle. Charged with passion he was indifferent to everything else and eyeing ravishingly the beauty of Rambha when the sage Durvasa, known for his very foul temper, happened to reach there. Indra was somewhat startled and habitually bowed in reverence to him. The sage was pleased and presented Indra a garland of the divine Paarijaat[3] flowers. But Indra's attention was directed to the beauteous body of Rambha and before he could accept the garland his passion was aroused once again. So much so, that he only casually accepted the garland and tossed it round the head of his favourite mount Airavat (the elephant). The elephant found the flowers's fragrance so overpowering that it began to dance. But as it shook its body, the garland was thrown off on the ground and was crushed under the elephant's feet.

All of this transpired before Durvasa could go out of the jungle. Durvasa is said to be Lord Shankar's Raudra (terrible) form's incarnation. Seeing the priced gift so ruthlessly trampled under the elephant's feet, he lost his temper and cursed Indra. "O Indra! How dare you insult the gift I so lovingly presented to you? Have you lost all your sense in the company of these vile women? Now I curse you that you shall be devoid of all prosperity and welfare. You shall start losing it like the moon loses its grace in the dark fortnight and no power in the world can restore it to you."

Indra was bewildered. He committed a sacrilege, that too, before the violent tempered sage, Durvasa. He was Lord Shiv's wrath personified, whose curse was immutable and deadly in effect. Immediately he fell at the feet of the sage, forgetting totally about the ravishing beauty of the Apsara. But despite his

---
3. The wish-fulfilling tree, also known as Kalpavriksha.

utter supplication and request to the sage to pardon him and reduce the intensity of the curse, Durvasa did not relent. Severely distressed, Indra at once started feeling depressed like a pauper. His face also lost its shine and his golden ornaments became as dead as a piece of wood. When Indra failed to placate the sage's foul temper, he fled in search of his guru Brihaspati who was lost in his meditation near the river Ganga.

Falling at his feet Indra narrated his tale of woe. The divine Guru also grew very angry at Indra : "How dare you act so blindly before the mighty sage? His curse is immutable and no body can alter its effect. It is like the curse of Destiny. You will have to suffer the consequences. No one can escape the consequence of one's deed, fair or foul, whether one is Chief of the gods or an ordinary being. Now only Narayan (Lord Vishnu) can help you. You must chant his Mantra for one lakh times. Meanwhile I consult Lord Brahma to see if he can suggest some means to approach Lord Vishnu."

So saying, Brihaspati took Indra to Lord Brahma who was besides himself with dismay and shock when he heard about Indra's temerity before the sage Durvasa. "How could you be so knaive or callous as to indulge in amorous dalliance before a high sage? Do you think you are par excellence because of your position as Indra? Shed off these notions! These sages and seers are those who actually decide as to who should be the chief of the gods, on the performance of his earlier deeds. By acting so foolishly you have not only lost your grace in this term of the position but also of the coming ones also."

When admonished by Brahma, Indra besought his forgiveness and promised that he would never insult any noble man. Then after Brahma advised him to pray Lord Vishnu for help as Shree Narayan (Vishnu) was the lone god in the entire universe who could protect the victim from the sage Durvasa's wrath. Chanting the "12 Matra Mantra": OM NAMO BHAGWATE VĀSUDEVĀYA, Indra followed Brahma and reached before

Lord Vishnu who was reclining upon his serpent coil. Having sang hymns to draw the Lord's attention, Indra narrated his tale of woe. Then Brahma requested Vishnu to help Indra as he was quite repentful and sorry. Lord Vishnu said : "Prosperity and good luck desert those who insult elders, show contempt to the ones who are adorable, who do not treat their uninvited guests with due care and hospitality; who show no respect to Brahmans and have no consideration for cows. Indra, you have committed a felony, a sacrilege. Even I cannot help you get back your lost glory and prosperity. But I can suggest a way by which you might get it back."

"Kindly enlighten me, Lord! I would do anything to get my prosperity and glory. I am prepared to undergo the severest possible penance to get it back. For without glory and prosperity I am finished for ever. Neither I could continue to be Indra for long nor I would get peace in any other species. So please enlighten me, My saviour," Indra was almost in tears when he supplicated so piteously.

"Lakshmi or Shree is all that is good and prosperous in the world. She is the net result of your achievements. The glow that comes on your face when you have achieved something you desiderated for long is the radiance of that Goddess, the aura of that diety. That Goddess, in her symbolic form is now hiding in the bottom of the ocean. If you could bring her out to the surface and worship her face to face, perhaps you would get back all that you have lost by the sage's curse. So you must arrange to have the Ocean churned. That is the only possible way of propitiating the Goddess."

Then with the support of all the gods and demons also, the Ocean was churned and the goddess eventually emerged on the moon-less night of Kartik's dark fortnight.[4] As the Goddess emerged, Indra chanted the Beej Mantra of the Goddess for a

---
4. The story has been given in details in the earlier chapter. The Amavasya is the day Deepavali is celebrated with lightinglamps.

million times and concluded his worship of the Goddess by singing reverentially the following hymn:

> Namah kamalavaasinyei naraayanyei namo namah
> Krishnapriyayei satatam Mahalakshmyei namo namah ǀ
>
> Aham yaavat tvayaa heenah bandhuheenashcha bhikshukah
> Sarvasampat-viheenashcha taavdeva Haripriye ǁ

[Meaning: O Dweller in the lotus, spouse of Narayan, the beloved of Vishnu, O Mahalakshmi! My repeated obeisance to you! O Mother Goddess! I am like a pauper if I don't receive your grace. All affluence would stay away from me—so shall be my all relations and friends. O Lord Vishnu's beloved spouse! Only your grace can ensure my prosperity and well-being once again. My all friends and relations could again be affectionate to me if I receive your blessings. Please help me, Mother! Only you can be my saviour!]

While reciting this hymn Indra grew so much charged with emotion that he began to cry like a child. Goddess Lakshmi was propitiated and she raised her hand to bless Indra, saying: "Don't cry, O Chief of gods! You shall ever get my grace and henceforth you shall ever be prosperous. I declare that all who chant this hymn to invoke me to get my blessing, shall do so without fail."

Thus redeeming Indra from that effect of that dire curse, Lakshmi went to Vaikuntha with Vishnu and all the gods chanted slogans in the honour of that great Goddess Lakshmi. Indra got back all that he had lost and happily went back to his capital Amarāvati.

(v) Yuddhishthir's Performing Goddess Lakshmi's Worship on the Advice of Lord Krishna

The Pandavas were roaming about dense jungles after losing their kingdom to the Kauravas in the gambling session in which their wicked cousin Duryodhan had cheated them. Those who were used to sleeping on silken-soft couches were forced to sleep on the naked earth; those who always had their choicest food in the golden ultensils were having raw fruits of jungles held in a bowl made of wild leaves! They felt truly deprived of every thing. They felt as though they have made the Goddess of riches and prosperity, Lakshmi, angry.

Once they were sitting in the jungle when Lord Krishna happened to visit them. Yudhishthir told him about their deprived life and solicited his advice as to what they should do to make the Goddess again shed her grace on them.

Lord Krishna said: "O Dharmaraja! Do not feel so depressed. This is just a temporary phase and soon you will be happy and prosperous. But in the meanwhile your brothers must continue to worship Lakshmi, especially on the Kartik Amavasya. There is an interesting story related to Lakshmi's worship on this day. Listen to it carefully as this glory of Goddess brings great rewards to the listener."

"Long long ago there was a demon-king named Bali who, unlike other demon kings, was quite noble and religious-minded. The people under his rule were quite happy and prosperous. He himself was a great devotee of Lord Vishnu." "Once he took a pledge that he would perform one hundred Ashwamedha yaggyas.[5] Since he had the requisite power, authority and resources, he had every right to perform the hundred yagyas. But had he done so he would have become the chief of the gods also as Indra is one who performs hundred Ashwamedha yagyas. When Bali had performed ninety nine yagyas, the chief of gods felt his position on the divine throne threatened. So he requested Lord Vishnu to help him retain his

---

5. This yagya has been accorded great importance in our scriptures. A horse consecrated with all holy rituals and left to move at will was followed by the royal army. Whatever territory the horse covered was deemed to have fallen under the King's authority and those who prevented the horse's movement were fought against. In the end the horse was brought back and sacrificed at the holy altar.

position or else the king of the demons was likely to become the head of the gods also. That situation would have created a great disturbancce in the cosmic order of the world. The distinction between the pious and the wicked would have vanished. In order to prevent Bali from creating such a disturbance, Vishnu decided to deceive Bali. Then he disguised himself as a dwarf Brahman, called Vaman, and reached the venue where Bali was preparing to perform his hundredth yagya. Since Bali was a renowned king, famous for his charaitable and kind hearted nature, it was said that no beggar ever left his gate empty handed. When Vaman reached the venue, Bali welcomed him with great hospitality and asked what he could do for the Brahman."Have your boon, whatever you please!" Detecting a streak of arrogance in Bali's this offer, Vishnu in Vaman form replied: "O Great king! My requirement is quite meagre. I just want the piece of land my three steps could measure. That's all".

"Bali was amused to hear such a trifle demand and said haughtily : "With pleasure, holy Brahman! Put your three steps anywhere you want and own the land covered by them." Then Vaman asked if he would ratify his promise in the usual way, i.e., by pouring water on the supplicant's hands, and Bali agreed. As the water fell on Vaman's hand he began to grow. His first stride covered the whole sky (heavens), the second the earth. Now he asked the king as to where should he put his third step. Bali offered his own head. Thus in a trice Bali lost his whole empire. But Lord Vishnu was quite pleased with Bali's fulfilling his promise even at the cost of sacrificing everything that he had. So the Lord asked Bali to have his boon. Then Bali said : "Lord, although I have lost everything to you, my request is only this that for first three days the whole earth may come again under my rule. These three days are the thirteenth day, the fourteenth day and the fifteenth day of the dark fortnight of the month of Kartik." [6]

---

6. Two days before the Deewali day and the Deewali day itself.

"Lord Vishnu responded with "So be it" but asked : "Why have you chosen these three days. Bali replied : "These three days are devoted to goddess Lakshmi. I want these three days to be spent in total worship of the Goddess. People should light lamps, invoke the goddess with full rituals and give alms to the poor and needy. If I get the authority for these three days only I would not be deprived of anything ever even if I am a pauper. So shall my people be."

Delighted at the King's boon, Lord Vishnu said "So be it. I happily grant this boon to you. Whosoever worships Lakshmi during these three days shall never be a victim of any adversity and privation." So saying the Lord departed.

"Thus, O Dharmaraja,' Lord Krishna advised Yuddhishthir, "You brothers must worship the Goddess with full ritual during these three days. I am sure with the Goddess's grace you shall get back your lost kingdom."

4. Goddess Lakshmi: In Folk Tales of India

Folk-tales of any region reveal the basic psyche of a race. Since Goddess Lakshmi is one of the very important deities of the Hindu pantheon and the divinity of material wealth and prosperity, she figures in a variety of folk tales of India. Her character in these folk tales is revealed quite vividly. Some of the selected tales are being given below.

(i) The Prudent Old Woman : [This is the folk-tale from Manipur region].

Long ago there ruled a king called Yashovarman in Manipur who was a very noble hearted person. He was quite intelligent himself and respected the intelligent persons. His wife was also a god-fearing lady and very pious. One day she went to take bath in her roof-top bathroom, leaving her 'Naulakha' ((worth nine lakh rupees necklace) in a niche on the roof itself. While she was taking bath, a kite happened to spot her necklace. Deeming it to be something edible she dived at it and flew away holding it in her beak.

When the queen emerged from the bathroom, she was shocked to see her precious necklace missing. She did not hear anyone coming on the roof either when she was taking bath. Now she was quite dismayed. "How could that necklace vanish when no one came on to the roof," she thought. "May be, this is the doing of some expert thief. He might have come stealthily and eloped with my favourite Naulakha."

According to the traditional set-up in the entire palace, no male was allowed to come to the ladies section. So she called her headmaid and ordered her to frisk every maid working there. But the intensive search gave her nothing, not even a clue. Then she went to the king and told all that had transpired.

The King summoned his royal astrologer and asked him to predict the position of the missing necklace on the basis of his 'Prashna Jyotish' (instant astrological calculation of the planetary movement). The king had already sent her sleuth to all directions. The astrologer predicted that the necklace was lying in the northerly direction but nobody would be able to get it. "It shall be brought to you, Lord, on the third day," he concluded "by the person who has received it accidentally."

Although somewhat relieved that his queen would be getting it back, the king was against leaving everything to the effect of the planetary movement. He sent his troops in the northerly direction under the command of his most trusted commander. "He who brings it back to me shall be handsomely rewarded. His all desires would be fulfilled," the king declared, giving them an added incentive.

But the soldiers continued to search in vain and returned dejectedly. They could not find any trace of the valuable necklace. They did combing operations all over but without any success. The king was quite restless himself and tried to console his wife, banking his faith on the royal astrologer's prediction.

The kite that had taken that necklace was flying merrily while trying to crush the pearls of the necklace between its beak. But the bird found it very hard and having no taste. While flying the kite spotted a dead serpent lying on the thatched roof of a hut. Dropping the necklace on that thatch she clutched the dead serpent and flew away.

That hut belonged to an old woman. Hearing the sound of something falling on the thatch of her hut, she came out. Seeing the necklace tucked on the top of her hut, she was delighted. As she brought that necklace inside her hut, she was somewhat worried. "Where I live is almost a deserted area, being at the fag end of the town. So far I had no fear of losing anything because I did not have anything precious. Now this necklace. It must be worth of a fortune and belonging to someone in the royal family," she said to herself.

While she was lost in her thoughts, she found a couple of wood-cutters returning to the settlement. She overheard them talking : "The queen had lost her 'Naulakha-Haar' and the king had announced handsome reward to anyone who brings it back to the queen."

Hearing this the old woman thought to herself, "Why shouldn't I return it to the queen. It is a burden on me. As it is I can't wear it in the open for the fear of losing it. If I go to sell it, I am likely to be caught after this public declaration of the award by the king. Maybe, the king might offer me a reward more useful to me than this 'Naulakha Haar.'"

So thinking, she tucked up the necklace into her clothes and went to the capital. While going she was all the time thinking as to what reward she must demand if the king asked her choice after her returning the necklace. 'Should I demand riches, palace and property?' She again asked herself. 'But all these things are ephemeral. If he could give me something which may guarantee my prosperity for ever.'

While still lost in her thoughts she found herself in the capital. Enquiring from the people, she managed to reach before the king's palace. She made the gate-keeper go to inform the king that "an old woman has come with something that the king has been searching for all this while."

Getting the hint, the king asked the gate-keeper to bring that old woman in. "Is it not the 'Naulakha Haar' your queen had lost recently," she asked, displaying the necklace to the king the moment she reached inside the court.

"Oh yes! It is that necklace," the king confirmed jubilantly as he examined the necklace. "Where did you get it?" he asked

The old woman then narrated the whole story behind her getting the necklace. The king was quite pleased not only with the honesty of the old woman but also telling the story truthfully. Delightedly he returned the necklace to his queen and asked the prudent woman as to what reward she expected.

"My expectation is only this," replied the woman : "On the eighth day is the festival of lights, Deewali. I want, on that holy day, that no one else should worship the Goddess Lakshmi excepting myself. All should send the oil, earthen pits for lighting the lamps and all the necessary material for the ritual worship of Lakshmi to my hut. I wish to worship the Goddess all alone that day."

The king was surprised at this most unusual demand. He was thinking that the old woman would demand riches, property, jewellery and money. But what she wanted was the right of exclusive worship of the Goddess Lakshmi on that auspicious day. The king's curiosity got better of him and he asked : "But why you wish to worship the Goddess all alone and deprive others of their holy right. Why don't you get some gold coins, property or money as your reward instead?"

"Because," replied the prudent woman: "I want to be assured of my continued prosperity all through my life. The scriptures say that one who worships the Goddess devotedly on Deewali night gets the blessings of the Goddess of prosperity which ensure one's being materially happy. If others also do the same, the goddess' blessings would be divided and then my share would be much less. By preventing others from worshipping Lakshmi I wish to ensure receiving the blessings of the Goddess in their entirety."

"But won't you allow even me to worship the Goddess that day?" the king asked. "I am sure you would not like to see your king becoming a pauper if deprived of the Goddess's blessings', he added, sentimentally.

Now the old woman was silent for a few moments. She couldn't dare say that she didn't care for the king and if she allowed the king the right to worship the goddess on Deewali her share in the blessing of the Goddess was likely to be reduced considerably. Then after a careful brooding she hit upon a novel idea. "Okay, I allow you the right to worship Goddess Lakshmi that day but only after I have worshipped her."

The king accepted her condition. Since that day, it is said, in Manipur the "Deepavali poojan" had always been the first right of an old woman. Even the king's turn used to come after that. But when the king worshipped the goddess his all subjects used to join him. Thus everybody received the Goddess's blessings, the old woman getting the 'lion's share.'

[The story in a subtle way highlights the importance of Goddess Lakshmi's worship on the Deepavali night which is traditionally believed to ensure the worshipper's prosperity for the entire year].

(ii) The Komati Way [This folk-tale is from Andhra Pradesh]

It is believed that if Goddess Lakshmi's blessings ensure prosperity, Goddess Alakshmi's presence signifies advent of the evil days and adversity. Alakshmi is said to be the Goddess of poverty. She is also called Jyeshthadevi. [Komati is the term for a crafty merchant in Telugu language.]

Long long ago Alakshmi and Lakshmi developed a bitter dispute as to who was more beautiful. Each gave her argument and the discussion went on for days and days. Not being able to resolve their issue both of them decided to seek the opinion of a Komati staying nearby to settle the issue.

Although the Komati was a very intelligent person, it became a serious problem for him to pronounce his judgement in the dispute between the divine sisters. His judgement was sure to displease one of them and each goddess's displeasure was bound to have dire consequences for the Komati. He knew that Lakshmi was more beautiful. But if he said so, then Alakshmi was sure to curse him with poverty. And if in order to please

Alakshmi if he declared her to be more beautiful than Lakshmi, the latter might deprive him all the wealth and riches. Thus his pronouncement was sure to harm him either way. To decide on his course of action, he requested both the sisters to give him a day's time. Both of them agreed.

The Komati thought over the matter. Unable still to decide what he should say, he decided to refer the matter to Lord Vishnu when he invoked him during his morning prayers. With this decision, he slept soundly. But by the grace of the Lord, he didn't need to wait till the dawn as the solution appeared to him in his sleep.

Next day morning, as he was ready for the day, he saw the two divine sisters approaching his house. Pretending to observe them closely and keenly he said : "O Alakshmi Devi! To be frank you look more beautiful when you turn back and walk away with elegance and grace. And, O Lakshmi Devi! Your appearance is a feast to the eye when you step forward. If both of you walk as I say, you would realise the truth of my words."

Hearing his judgement both of them were very pleased. Komati had given his verdict on their dispute so laconically that each had the impression as though the Komati was praising her only.'Thus the brainy Komati not only solved that apparently impossible problem but managed to receive the blessings of both the sisters.

[If in a dispute one conducts oneself without leaning on either side, without uttering the real facts and without harming to one's own interest, it is known as the Komati way in Andhra Pradesh.]

(iii) Goddess Lakshmi's Promise

Once while resting on his lotus bed in the company of his consort, Lord vishnu said : "I feel like going to the planet earth and seeing the condition there with my own eyes."

"Yes Lord," agreed Lakshmi and added: "I shall also accompany you. Long time has elpsed since I last visited the earth. Let us see how people are faring there."

Lord Vishnu acceded to the request and in no time both of them found themselves beneath a peepul tree. After resting for a while to freshen themselves, Lord Vishnu said: "Now you rest here, my beloved, as I am going out to make a surprise visit. I don't want to take you along as I want to have a glimpse of the world first.'

After much persuasion he could make Lakshmi stay there. Leaving for his errand, he warned : "Lakshmi, while you stay here, you should not look towards south."

"Why Lord? Lakshmi questioned.

"Because I have been told by the divine priest Brihaspati that looking south might bode ill-luck for you." Lord explained.

"As you wish," Lakshmi said. Then Lord Vishnu went away and she, sitting beneath the Peepul tree began to pass her time by singing songs.

Suddenly it dawned upon her that there must be some other reason of the Lord's preventing her to look due south "What if I do look," Lakshmi asked herself, "After all! I am not so young and immature that I should be guided to look in which particular direction. I am here to see the world with my own eyes. I want to see in all directions. Who is he to put restrictions on my viewing the world?"

Thus thinking she looked towards the south. She was amazed to see a substantial number of the yellow mustard flowers. They looked so enchanting that she could not help going near them. She reached there and started dancing with joy amidst the fields. Decorating herself with those flowers she began to roam about merrily. As she ventured into the other field she found ripe sugar canes quite tempting. Pulling out a few stems from them she began to enjoy their juice with gay abandon.

While she was munching the third stem of the sugarcanes she saw Lord Vishnu approaching. Seeing her not only looking at but going to due south and enjoying herself with flowers and the sugar cane juice, the Lord became angry. "You must suffer for your disobedience. You have committed a crime. It is sin to disobey your husband. Now you will have to live in a farmer's house as a bonded labour for twelve years."

Lakshmi felt as though she had lost her power of speech. Meekly she followed the Lord's command and went to a farmer's house as an ordinary labourer to work in his fields for twelve long years. While she remained there for the stipulated period, the farmer noticed substantial growth in his prosperity. He was not aware of the identity of the person working in his field.

After the completion of the bonded period, she waited for Lord Vishnu and begged the farmer to release her. But farmer would not allow her to leave. "Your company with my family has made us quite prosperous. How can I allow you to leave and scuttle my chances of continued prosperity."

By that time Lord Vishnu also arrived and requested the farmer to release Lakshmi. But the farmer refused to oblige. For long the tussle between both the parties continued. At last Lord Vishnu suggested a via media. "We can stay here a bit more if you go to the holy Ganges and take bath there. On your return we shall leave. In your absence we would not leave."

Seeing the firmness at Lord Vishnu's face about the offer, the farmer had no go but to accept the offer. As he was about to leave, Lakshmi handed over four small shells or 'cowries' to the farmer for offering them to the Ganges. The farmer left with his family and had the holy dip in the divine river. As the farmer's wife threw those cowries into the water, she was surprised to see four hands emerging from the river and accepting the cowrie quite gratefully. The farmer, seeing the image of a very comely face on the Ganga surface, asked the river : "O Mother Ganga! Who has offered you these cowrie? Do you know her?" "She is Goddess Lakshmi? Don't you know this?" The farmer heard a voice emerging from the water. "What, Goddess Lakshmi," the farmer was amazed. "It was the Goddess who has all through been working in my field as an ordinary labourer," he said to himself, adding "No wonder my prosperity was growing ever since." But to confirm it he again asked: "Are you sure, Mother? She has been working in my fields for last twelve years."

"Yes, I am," the river replied. "She is Goddess Lakshmi. Don't let her leave your house," the rippling waves of the river asserted.

The farmer was delighted to have this information. When they returned home, the farmer requested Lakshmi not to leave them. But Lord Vishnu objected. "You can't keep Lakshmi bound to your house. She cannot make any house her permanent abode. She is by nature steady and fickle. Since she has completed her stay in your house, she must leave."

But the farmer was still adamant. He fell at Lord Vishnu's feet and supplicated repeatedly: "O Lord! Please! Let her stay in my house. Now I would not treat her like an ordinary labourer but shall worship her."

Seeing the farmer's great affection for her, Goddess Lakshmi intervened: "Look Dear! It is my destiny to roam about. I cannot remain bound to one house. But this I promise that he who devoutly performs my Pooja especially on the Kartik Amavasya Day and keeps darkness away from his house, I shall definitely visit his house at least once in a year, to ensure prosperity to that house. Now I must leave. But if you invoke me on that day I shall come again with a gift of a fortune for you."

So saying, the Goddess left with Lord Vishnu. The farmer bade them a tearful adieu. But now he was not sad. He knew how to invoke the Goddess' blessing. Since the Amavasya was falling next month, he had his house cleaned thoroughly. On the appointed day, he lighted so many lamps in his house that darkness was nowhere visible. The Goddess came and blessed him. Since then it has become customary to celebrate that day with lighting lamps and worshipping the Goddess. As she had promised, she comes that day to bless her worshippers. [This story is found in many folk tales of North India].

(iv) Goddess Lakshmi Curtails Lord Vishnu's Sleep

After the Ocean-churning when Lakshmi married Lord Vishnu, she thought her spouse must be active all the time as he had been known to be the ace trouble-shooter for the gods. But she found him relaxing most of the time on the serpent coil and frequently dozing. His these periods stretched to quite long duration, leaving Lakshmi all alone to manage their abode.

Unable to put up with the situation any more, she one day complained to the Lord : "My Master! I am not happy the way you sleep. This you do quite frequently and for centuries together. Thus I have to suffer very long separation from you even when you are close to me. Without your guidance it is difficult to manage affairs here. Many sages and gods come and every time I have to request them to wait. If you remember, a few centuries ago when the sage Bhrigu came, he cursed you when you were found not available for performing your required duty."

"Yes I do," interrupted the Lord rather irritably, being unable to decipher the purpose of his espouse's rather long sermon. "What are you driving at ?"

"I am requesting that you must discipline your schedule. You know, you have always a stream of gods, the sages and even humans waiting for your Darshan. They come and stay here for months and years with the hope that you may get up one day. Most of them return rather disappointed. But I can't help. I cannnot allow them in your bed-chamber when you are asleep. Perhaps you are not aware that during the period you remain asleep many negative forces surface in the world. Then you have to incarnate yourself on the earth to remove them. My request is this: Why should you sleep so frequently and for such a long period to allow these evil forces to raise up their head. If you remain awake, may be, the need for your incarnation does not even arise."

"May be, you are right," Lord Vishnu agreed, seeing much sense in what the Goddess was saying. "You know, to take Avataar (Incarnation) is to go down and suffer the mortal ills, albiet temporarily."

"Yes Lord," Lakshmi exclamied rather emphatically, adding: "That is why I say that you must curtail your sleep and look at the world below more frequently. As you say Incarnation involves some difficulty even to your goodself. Let you nip the bud of these evil forces early so that they might not advance to alarming proportions. You must schedule your time better and curtail your slumber hours to the bare minimum."

Lord Vishnu realised his lapse. He gave a very patient hearing to Goddess Lakshmi. He consoled her and said he appreciated her difficulty. Henceforth he would try to mend his habit."

That very moment the messenger brought in the news that a delegation of the gods was waiting at the gate to meet the Lord. Lord Vishnu ordered him to let the gods come in.

The gods, led by their chief, Indra, were rather perplexed. Reaching near they said to Lord Vishnu: "O Almighty! Daitya (Demon) Shankhayan[1] has assumed great power. He wants to deprive people of knowledge. He has stolen the Vedas, the treasure of our immortal knowledge. Please retrieve the Vedas from the nether world."

Lord Vishnu assured them that soon he would retrieve the Vedas. It was learnt later that the Demon had been given a boon by the creator on the strength of which he had become so much powerful.

Lord Vishnu immediately went to the netherworld to search for the demon. He took no time to spot the dreaded devil.

---
1. Some stories link this folk-tale with Lord Vishnu's Boar Incarnation and call this demon Hiranyaaksha.

The Lord chased the demon, fought a very long battle against him and brought the Vedas back to the world.

The people were jubilant to receive their holy books. They rejoiced the occasion. Having retrieved the Vedas and entrusting them into Lord Brahma's custody, Lord Vishnu said : "I am tired after a long bout with the devil. I want rest. Now I will sleep."

As he said so, Lakshmi's heart missed a beat. She thought that the Lord might relapse into his favourite habit. So, in order to remind the Lord of his earlier promise to her, Lakshmi quickly asked: "How long, Master?"

Lord Vishnu was startled for a moment, then realising the cause of Lakshmi's apparent worry, replied with a smile: "Today is the eleventh day of Ashadh.[2] I will limit my sleep now to just four months only. Now I shall retire on my lotus bed floating in the Milky ocean. Its waves will lull me to sleep. I shall break my sleep on the eleventh day of Kartik."

Although the time of Lord's sleep was quite curtailed, Lakshmi was still not satisfied. She wanted to get assurance from the Lord that nothing untoward would happen during the period Lord slept. So, very clearly she asked again : "Master ! What should the people do during these four months?"

Lord Vishnu replied : "The people should pass this time by observing fasts. They should take light food in these four months. This period will be mostly covered by the rainy season on the earth. It is likely to induce sleep and dullness in their body and hence give rise to various diseases and negative forces. So, they must avoid sleeping during the day time. Simple diet, regulated living, prayers, attending the holy discourses, reading scriptures and regular exercise should be resorted to. Only then they would feel no trouble during the period. Also, they should not observe any special ceremony like marriages etc., during this period as I won't be awake myself to bless the young couple. If they follow

---

[2]. Mid-June to Mid-July.

this regimen no one would suffer any affliction and disease. shall be pleased with those who adhere to my this advice."

So saying, Lord Vishnu retired. Lakshmi was happy that her Master acceded to her request. Since then these four months are not considered right time for any sacred ceremony. The day Lord Vishnu wakes up is known as Devuthaan Ekadashi which is still considered to be a very auspicious day in most of the north India. [This folk tale with colloquial variations appears in most of the states of the Northern India].

(v) Goddess Lakshmi: A Deity Kind to the Humble

One upon a time there lived a poor rustic named Pingala in a village. He had a large family but not resources to support it. His wife was a religious lady who regularly did a devout worship to Goddess Lakshmi but the Goddess had not responded to her prayers. Since Pingala had no other means of earning a livelihood to support his large family, he used to go to the nearby forest, cut wood and earn his bread by selling it. One day when he was on his way to the forest with his axe on his shoulder, it started drizzling which soon developed into a heavy downpour. He ran to find a dry place. As he was searching for shelter he found a wooden pavilion and entered it. He stayed there for some time but there seemed no end to the rain. Though he found temporary relief in the shelter of the pavilion, he was quite perturbed as to what his family would eat thay day. If he went home empty handed how would he face his hungry children. "Poor kids!" he thought to himself : "It is your sheer bad luck to be born in my house. I can't even provide you one square meal." Though he was quite depressed at the prospect of returning home empty handed, his eyes were still searching for some dry wood in their last ditch attempt. Suddenly his grief striken eyes saw a stout wooden pillar planted in the middle of the pavilion. It was an image of the Goddess Lakshmi carved in wood.

Looking at the pillar, he was delighted and muttered to himself: "God is great. He does not allow anyone to die of starvation. There are thousands means of his providing food for everyone. Just when I was crying for want of resources to feed my family this wooden pillar has appeared before me. It is not only stout but quite dry. I can get a full load of fuel out of it. Since it is raining I might fetch double of the price for my this dry wood." So ecstatically he lifted his axe and was about to strike it at the pillar when with a booming voice, the Goddess Lakshmi appeared in person ; "Stop it, you fool! How dare you strike me? Don't you know I am Goddess Lakshmi?"

Pingala was bewildered with a shock. The axe fell from his hand. Trembling in fear he prayed with folded hands: "O Mother Goddess! Pardon me! Save me! It was in sheer ignorance I was about to strike the axe at your image. I thought it was an ordinary pillar planted here by some one. Please pardon me! Had I known, would I dare commit such sacrilege?" He immediately prostrated himself before the Goddess in utter supplication. The Goddess felt pity and gently lifted him. Then he told her his entire tale of woe, hearing which the Goddess said : "Now shed off your fear as I have pardoned you. I am sorry to know about your such a misearble condition. Now listen. You shall always be satisfied henceforth. Your no want shall remain unfulfilled. Go home, have a bath, clean the kitchen, bring new pots, place them on the hearth and cover them. You will find all sorts of foodstuff that you desire when you remove the cover on the pots. You and your children will always eat to your hearts' content by repeating this ritual every day. But don't give out this secret to anyone. Now you may return home." And so saying the Goddess disappeared.

Pingala was besides himself with joy. He threw away his axe and went home rejoicing. When his wife and children saw him coming empty handed, their heart sank. But before his wife could say anything, he becalmed them. Then he took his wife to a corner and narrated her the whole incident. Overwhelmed with joy she hastened to bring the new pots. She cleaned her kitchen thoroughly and did exactly as Pingala asked her to do. Covering the new pots with the lids they sat around and remembered the Goddess. Then they removed the lids. Lo and behold! They had the choicest dishes they ever wanted to enjoy. Some of which were only names to them as they had not even seen them hitherto. They partook of their meals delightedly. Thenceforth this became a daily routine with them. They ate heartily but the food supplied was not only rich in quality but ample in quantity also. They began to distribute it to their friends and relatives almost everyday.

Their next door neighbour was Mandodari, a cantankerous termagent. Her vile temper was known to everyone. She was quite jealous by nature. Watching the plenitude and happiness of Pingala family she grew curious and thought to herself. "These people used to come to my door very often for some loan of rice and oil. Now there appears to be no scarcity in their house. But there is no indication that they are purchasing anything from outside. Still they manage to not only eat sumptuously but distribute the food to others as well. How are they able to do so? I must find the cause of their sudden prosperity."

So thinking, one day she invited Pingala's eight year old son to her house. Then she asked about how they managed their affairs so nicely. "I don't even see your mother cooking anything. The other day I saw her standing out and chatting till late in the evening. Then I heard you want food and she procured it as if by magic. How do you all manage to get everything. Now you seem to be quite rich."

This boy was a friend of Mandodari's son who always bragged about his riches. Now when Mandodari said to Pingala's son that "You people seem to be quite rich," the boy felt elated and disclosed everything that he heard his father telling his mother.

Now Mandodari thought herself to be singly unfortunate as she had to pass through the drudgery of cooking meals everyday. But she thought that now since she knew how to get rid of this every-day trouble, she would force her husband to repeat all that Pingala had done to get this boon from the Goddess. As soon as her husband returned from the market where he had his shop and asked for some food, Mandodari spoke harshly to him and said that she would not cook food or do anything thereafter. Shocked at her behaviour he asked the children whether any thing had happened during his absence. They said that she had been behaving like that since Pingala's son told her something. When he asked her what the matter was, she narrated all that she had heard from that boy. Then she ordered her husband to go to the forest and strike at Goddess Lakshmi's image to get the desired boon.

Her husband was equally surprised. He pondered over the matter coolly and said: "My dear! Gods grant boons to the devotees who pray but not to those who threaten. Do you know this?" Now Mandodari blew up. "How could you dare give me sermons?" She asked threateningly and began to throw and break old pots and utensils to express her anger. "Things can be achieved through fear and not by pleading or begging. Do not entertain doubts. Now either You would do as I have instructed you or I would not cook any food. I don't care even if my own children die of hunger but I would not cook any food now. Go and get the boon. Only then you can have food."

At last her husband agreed to do so. During the night she bought a big axe for her husband. Early in the morning when he was about to depart she again reminded him of the instructions in greater details. Her final instruction was: "Ask the Mother Goddess only the eatables and nothing else. Everything else can be bought but cooking food," she said disdainfully, "is an anathema to me. I want only to be relieved of the daily drudgery of cooking. Now go and do exactly as I have advised you."

The henpecked husband had no alternative but to go to the forest and threaten to seek the Goddess's blessing. After much roaming about he managed to find the pavilion of the Goddess. Entering he saw the wooden image of the Goddess and lifted his axe to strike it. Roaring like the thunder, the Goddess appeared before him and catching hold of his tuft of hair she gave him a severe beating. The Goddess's this violent behaviour was quite unexpected. His wife had also not given any hint about the Goddess's murderous mood. Screaming and weeping he pleaded that he did not do this of his own accord, but because of his wife's persuasion. The Goddess exploded in anger: "You fool! Pingala is a poor wreck. He had tried to strike at the image quite ignorantly, not pronouncingly like you tried to do. I have sympathy for the hapless paupers like Pingala but not for you. You say it was your wife's plan. All right. I had forgotten to give Pingala two measures of Ghee. Poor fellow must be consuming edibles dry, without ghee. If you agree to supply two measures of ghee to Pingala everyday, I will free you— otherwise I will kill you. You can't escape my wrath. Now what do you say?" the Goddess asked threateningly.

The poor fellow was trembling with fear. He immediately agreed to supply two measures of ghee to Pingala to escape death at the Goddess' hand. Then the goddess Lakshmi freed him with a warning of severe consequences if he did not keep his promise and gave him a violent push which landed him direct into the courtyard of his own house.

While he was having the violent Darshan of the Goddess, Mandodari was expectantly cleaning her house with great enthusiasm and decorating it with festoons and 'Satia' (auspicious figures) made on the gate. She was so sure of her husband returning with the desired boon that she had already purchased new pots and utensils including their covers. She wanted no time wasted in the preparation to realise the effect of the boon. Moreover, as she didn't cook that night, she and her children, both, were quite hungry. Owing to severe hunger it was difficult for them to even sleep. They were eagerly waiting to receive the happy message that the Goddess had granted the boon.

Looking to their unusual activity in the late hours of night, Mandodari's neighbours got curious and asked her: "Why this such unusual activity? Do you have something important coming up in the morning ?"

"No," replied the shrewed lady. In her attempt to ward the curious neighbours off, she added. "In fact after a couple of days we propose to throw a ceremonial party to celebrate my son's birthday. I am tidying up the house a bit. You see, the domestic chores hardly leave anytime to do these things." Then after a pause she said again : "And please don't forget to attend that party. I shall give you the advance information." In fact she wanted to say that the feast she was referring about might take place the very next day but she checked herself. She wanted to be doubly sure. So she began to eagerly wait for her husband. The children could not resist sleep and sprawled themselves on the floor and slept. Now Mandodari was waiting for her husband alone.

When it was almost dawn and her husband didn't turn up, she peeped out in the courtyard to see whether the day was breaking or not. In the slight pre-dawn light she spotted something lying supine in her courtyard. Curiosity got better of her and she rushed out to find her husband lying in the courtyard. His face and limbs were swollen and he was unconscious. She rushed to fetch water and sprinkled it on her husband's face. Slowly he opened his eyes, groaning with pain. She was shocked to see her husband in such a bad shape. "What happened to you? Couldn't you meet the Goddess?" she asked. "You are so devil," he replied with great difficulty. "You never listen to me. You have such a wile temper, bad tongue and stubborn behaviour. When I said we cannot extract boons from gods by threatening them, you bragged. See how severely the Goddess beat me, when

I lifted the axe to strike at her image. The Goddess said clearly that she always helped the real poors and not impostors like me. She not only thrashed me physically but forced me to agree to give two measures of ghee daily to Pingala as she herself had forgotten to grant him. It was only on my accepting to supply two measures of ghee daily to our neighbour that she spared me. Now if we don't fulfil this condition of the Goddess, we shall suffer very dire consequences. The Goddess had given me a clear warning."

Hearing all this Mandodari flared up and said : "My foot! Huh! Why should give two measures of ghee to Pingala? I am not afraid of any divinity. Let the Goddess come here. I will see what she does. She does not know me. It is only your timidity which led her to impose this condition on us. I care two hoots for that." So saying she began to loudly abuse the Goddess.

While she was straining her vocal chords to puke out choicest abuses, she felt a severe stomach ache and her stomach began to swell. In no time it swelled as much as to be of the size of a big pitcher. She started yelling in great pain and fear. Hearing her cries the neighbours also gathered there and learnt the cause of her trouble. They forced Mandodari to obey the divine order, saying that the Goddess was not a human being to be daunted by her bad tongue. At last the helpless Mandodari had to obey the divine order and gave two measures of ghee to Pingala. As soon as she did so her stomach became normal and the pain vanished. Whenever she delayed in supplying ghee to Pingala she faced this trouble. Soon she realised her mistake and began to worship the Goddess as Pingala's wife did. Then after a year's worship, the Goddess was propitiated and gave Mandodari also the boon of prosperity. Though Mandodari prospered, she had to continue cooking, as the Goddess refused to grant her the boon she had given to Pingala.

5. The Ritualistic Worship of Goddess Lakshmi

As mentioned earlier, Deepawali or Deewali is the day (or night) of Goddess Lakshmi's special worship. Although the Goddess is said to grant prosperity and riches, yet if we observe the pre-requisites of her worship, we realise that she is also the Goddess of cleanliness. No other deity's worship requires such a massive cleaning of the entire house—not only of the special chamber of worship. People clean their houses around Deewali with special enthusiasm to welcome Lakshmi, they remove the dirt, old clothes, torn garments etc. They have their house whitewashed and freshly painted. Getting new clothes, new shoes etc., is an age old custom.

Although the Indian concept of hygiene and cleanliness lays much emphasis on the personal hygiene, it is not so rigid for the public hygiene. Such scenes are very common in India in which a devout person, taking bath at least four times during a day, is spitting merrily at his neighbour's wall or right below his own house. Such persons do not consider their these acts as being unhygienic or even uncivil. This is in direct contradiction to the western concept of hygiene wherein more emphasis is laid on the public hygiene. One may wonder at the neat and clean roads, markets, public building in the western countries but one hardly find a western taking bath regularly. May be these styles of living or the very ethical values are determined by the climatic conditions of a particular region or even a country. More emphasis on personal hygiene in India has probably resulted out of the tropical conditions prevalent here. Constant perspiring at least for ten months, the atmospheric dirt and the dry dust of the ground have been jointly responsible for making one take bath at least once everyday in India. Since these are more or less absent in the western climes, bathing is not that necessary.

But at the time of Deepawali, even Indians become conscious of general unhygienic conditions. The reason is two fold. Since the onset of the month Kartik heralds the best period in the Northern India with pleasant, mild winter replacing the hot and humid rainy season and Nature appears as spick and span as a freshly bathed dame, people try to match that cleanliness by cleaning their environs. They clean their houses, their roads, their markets, decorate them with a touch of cultural aesthetics and do all that they ought to do all the year round. These operations have some overtones of the medical requirements. As has been the style of the Hindu tenets, mixing religion with social or individual requirement is quite apparent around this time. Whitewashing of the houses around this time is an age old custom. It is done precisely for two reasons : One is the result of an individual's natural desire to invite prosperity in the form of Lakshmi and the other is owing to a medical requirement. One reason has already been discussed in details in the earlier chapter. Only the second one would be dilated upon.

India, being a tropical country, has a long spell of rains. When this season is over, the rains stop but humidity remains. This humidity seeps down the walls of the houses, causing the walls to sweat which also become the breeding ground for a variety of insects and mosquitoes. Owing to stale air and very well pronounced humidity, these germs cause an outbreak of a variety of illnesses and viral fevers. This season, called 'Sharad' in Sanskrit is the most difficult period to survive. Hence the popular maxim "Jeeven Sharadah Shatam" or let us live for hundred 'Sharad' seasons. The inherent assertion is that if one survives through 'Sharad', One is sure to live for the rest of the year. The reckoning point is Sharad and not other seasons like 'Shishir' or 'Vasant'. Owing to the great natural disturbance caused by the rains, the next season gets full of germs and viruses. So one has to live very cautiously through this season. Having only one principal meal during the first fortnight after the rains or during the 'Shraddha Paksha' and having virtually no solid food during the coming nine days or during the 'Navratras' are some of the measures one has to adopt to survive through this difficult period. Besides taking these health-oriented measures, one has to get the surroundings also cleansed of the dirt, dust and germs. So around Deewali, people not only clean their houses but also have their houses whitewashed to remove the inherent humidity that seeps down the 'marrow' of the walls. The solution that is used to whitewash the houses has ample dose of lime—the natural dehumidifying agent. This coating of lime ensures the absorption of all the residual humidity inside the houses and thus the breeding ground for the germs and insects is also removed. Hence the prevalent custom of whitewashing the houses before Deewali.

The celebration of the Deewali Day starts from early morning. People get up early in the morning, tidy up their houses which have already been white-washed, decorate the arches with festoons and other means, take their bath and then go to the market to buy the earthen lamps, cotton wicks, oil etc. In the evening they place the earthen lamps filled with oil and fixed with the cotton wicks. They have special meals prepared on this occasion. Gifting sweet packets and other items are also part of the Deewali custom. Having done all these preparations they eagerly wait for the auspicious hour which is determined by astrological calculations.

The worship of Lakshmi starts with cleaning the place or the temple with pious Gangajal and the sacred cowdung. Then on the high pedestal a joint image of Lakshmi and Ganesh is installed. Some people have these images made of mud and colours while the elite class get these images specially carved in gold or silver. The following material is required for Lakshmi worship: the two stems of the banana tree, a bunch of the mango leaves (minimum five), the golden (or mud) image of the Goddess Lakshmi, a well cleaned metal pitcher, a piece of the sacred thread or the yagyopaveeta, five gems (depending upon the financial capability of the worshipper), a piece of silken garment, grains of rice, a piece of camphor, incense, a garland of flowers, five leaves of the basil (Tulsi) plant, a piece of wood apple, a betel leaf, the freshly produced and partially roasted rice grains (called 'kheelen), peculiar sweet-objects known as Khilonas[1], Panchamrita (made by mixing curds, milk, ghee, honey, sugar and a few leaves of the basil plants), fruits, saffron, holy red string, festoons, a wooden pedestal, and a coconut shell.

Having cleaned the place, instal the joint image of Lakshmi and Ganesh on it. Place the metal pitcher, covering it with the mango leaves and placing the coconut shell on the cover of it. The pitcher should be kept alongside the banana stem covered with the piece of red garment. All these things should be kept before the Goddess including the edibles and Panchamrita. The process of worship differs from place to place and region to region. But here we are giving the one most prevalent in north India. In the Prasadam of the Goddess, the 'Kheelen' and Khilona or Batāsha have especial significance as these represent the agriculture produce.

Many people start worship with lighting an earthen lamp filled with ghee. Then the deities' foreheads are marked with the holy vermilion powder (or Roli) and the rice grain. In some regions they mark the forehead with a gold coin or the gold ornament. After marking the deities with the holy powder, the ghee filled burning lamp is moved around the deities with the accompaniment of the Goddess's Arti preceded by Ganesh Vandana. Then they partake of the prasadam in the form of Kheelen etc; fruits and Panchamrita. As soon as the worship is over the priest or the head of the family marks the forehead of the other members of the family with the holy mark. It is customary to light lamps placed in readiness over the sills and the boundary walls of the house. When all the earthen lamps have been lighted the younger ones start bursting the crackers and the elders go to greet their friends and relatives. In some communities, calling

---

1. These are made of raw sugar or khandasari sugar and moulded in peculiar shapes resembling animals.

on their bereaved relatives and sending sweets etc., is the ritual reserved for the Diwali day. The idea is to cheer up those sorrowing persons and make them eat the sweets etc., as they themselves would not prepare owing to the bereavement in their family. The ghee-filled lamp is kept on burning for the entire night and the soot collected in the lamp is applied as collyrium in the eyes the following morning. It is essential to place a candle or an earthen lamp near the exhaust-points in the house. The folk-belief says that all the inlets of the house should be kept properly lighted for this Goddess of Prosperity's entry into the house.

In some families gambling is part of the Deewali celebrations. They believe that through gambling they test their financial luck for the rest of the year. Victory in these gambling sessions is heralded as the sure sign of the imminent prosperity.

Besides Deewali, in some regions a festival called 'Kojagara' is also celebrated to propitiate the Goddess of Prosperity, Lakshmi. This festival is observed on the night of full moon in the month of Ashwina.[2] 'Kojagara' literally means the night of awakening. It is also a festival of Goddess Lakshmi, who descends on the earth on this auspicious night to bless all with health and prosperity—specially those who remain awake the entire night. This is one of the most popular festivals of the Central India—especially the Bundelkhand region. In order to remain awake the people pass this entire night singing and dancing, chanting hymns and orisons to draw the Goddess's attention.

It is also a harvest festival and is celebrated throughout the country in one form or the other. Lakshmi is worshipped and night vigil is observed. According to a folk tale a king, on his queen's advice worship the Goddess on this night when he had fallen on the evil days and by the Goddess' grace he recovered his lost kingdom. This festival's celebration involves no ritual worship but confined to invoking the Goddess by singing hymns and devotional songs.

---

2. Mid Sept. to Mid October, according to Gregorian calendar.

6. Famous Temples of Goddess Lakshmi

As mentioned earlier, Goddess Lakshmi is not worshipped alone but always in the company of her spouse Lord Vishnu. All the famous temples which have Lakshmi's idol are called Lakshmi Narayan temples. Though there are scores of temples dedicated to this divine couple, we shall be discussing about those which are well known.

(i) Lakshmi Narayan Temple, Delhi

One of the most famous shrines located in the heart of the capital city, it is a modern Hindu Temple constructed by the ace industrialist family, the Birlas in 1938. It is situated west of Connaught Place on Mandir Marg and believed to be the most beloved shrine for the worshippers of the Goddess of prosperity. The temple houses life size images of Narain and his consort Lakshmi, the goddess of wealth. On special days or festival it becomes the cynosure of all devotees of Delhi region.

(ii) Lakshmi Narain Temple, Mathura-Vrindavan

This temple was also constructed by the Birla family in the thirties of the current century and hence quite modern. It is situated on Mathura-Vrindavan Marg, about midway between the two holy places. The images are carved so aesthetically that they almost look live. Situated amongst the picturesque surroundings teeming with greenery this shrine is easily approachable by countless means of transport plying between the two holy centres of the Krishna cult.

(iii) Lakshmi Narain Temple, Jaipur

Inside the city of Jaipur, near Moti Doongari stands this majestic and magnificent temple dedicated to Lakshmi-Narayan. This was also constructed by the Birla family and it is comparatively of recent origin. The towering temple built on an elevation and set in spacious lawns can be seen from miles around. The curvilinear white marble shikhar (apex) of the shrine soaring high into the sky, looks like a ballad in stone when viewed in floodlights in the evening.

(iv) Lakshmi Narayan Temple, Ellora Caves

The Ellora caves, carved out in a sickle shaped hill, are 30 kms. from Aurangabad. These caves have statues and idols belonging to almost all faiths, the Hindu, Buddha, Jain faiths. There are about 17 caves which are devoted to Hindu gods and goddesses. Specially the cave no. 14 contains quiet a good number of those Hindu Divine images. There is an old idol of Lord Vishnu together with his consort Lakshmi. To reach these idols the best course is to reach Aurangabad which is well connected by air, rail and road with major cities, and has good hotels etc., also.

(v) Mahalakshmi Temple, Bombay

It is perhaps the only shrine which is exclusively dedicated to Lakshmi, the goddess of riches. It is situated down the Malabar Hill, further along the coast. It is the image of the most revered goddess of Bombay.

In most of these idols or images the goddess is represented with four arms but more often only with two. In some pictures Goddess Lakshmi is also shown seated with Lord Vishnu on the divine eagle, named Garuda, holding a snake in its claws. In some of the images she is depicted holding a lotus in her hand which suggests wealth in the form of water which can be so precious in India's climate. Lakshmi-Narayan are conveniently grouped with Lord Vishnu supporting Lakshmi with one of his left arms (as he is invariably showed with four arms) and Lakshmi having her right arm round his shoulders.

Whatever the representation, this Goddess is invoked to bless the devotee with good things of life. Her figure is sometimes depicted on the floors of home to bring good luck and to drive away evil influences. Interestingly enough bad luck is personified as Alakshmi or Jyesthadevi, the sister of Lakshmi. In Bengal goddess Lakshmi is depicted on earthen vessels and worshipped on the day just after the Durga Puja. She is often worshipped in a basket or a pot used as corn measure, painted red. This basket or pot is decorated with flower. As the same is filled with unhusked rice she manifests herself in the shape of the seedlings grown in the winnowing basket.

The popular representation of the Goddess in the company of Lord Vishnu is meant to convey the unified concept of power and energy. Vishnu is the representation of that power which sustains the world and Lakshmi represents the inherent energy in that power. Both are inseparable. Hence the joint image of Lakshmi and Narain.

Another reason behind this joint representation is the traditional Hindu concept that material wealth alone is an evil and leads the way to hell. The denigration of wordly riches has been a favourite topic with all the holy books of the Hindu Dharma including the much revered book 'Gita'. According to our ancient seers and thinkers there is no end to the greed for material wealth hence it should not be pursued or fulfilled. It has a tendency to grow on what it is fed. One can get away from this yearning only be renouncing it.

But the use of the material wealth cannot be gainsaid. It is as necessary as oxygen to life to survive in this world. It is to accept this fact that this Goddess of wealth has been associated with the Sustainer of the world, i.e., with Lord Vishnu. The inherent message in their association is : that material wealth is auspicious which is used for the welfare of the entire world. Since wealth alone is deemed dangerous, there is hardly any separate temple of the Goddess and she is mostly adored as the consort of Lord Vishnu.

Although Lakshmi is also worshipped with Ganesh at Deewali, there is no temple having joint images of Lakshmi and

Ganesh. It appears that their association at Deewali is purely a temporary affair. They are together only at Deewali but not any other time. This fact, again, gives credence to the theory that Lord Ganesh was initially not a deity of the Aryan goddom but was adopted later when the Aryan and the Dravidians developed cordial relations between themselves. So, when Ganesh became a deity for the Aryans, he was temporarily associated with Lakshmi for the simple reason that he should remove all the hurdles that come in one's way of getting the Goddess's blessing. Ganesh joining Lakshmi signifies the eternal desire of man who always craves for material wealth without any impediment. The Lord of all impediments or Vighneshwar was associated with the Goddess of prosperity for this reason by the ancient seers.

This appears quite plausible because there is no reference in our scriptures or mythological literature about Vishnu's any association with Ganesh. Of course it was Vishnu who procured the elephant-head when Lord Shiv had beheaded Ganesh unknowingly but that is the end of their association. There is no reference either of Lakshmi's any special association with Ganesh barring their joint worship at Deewali.

Even in Deewali images, Ganesh is always depicted having Lakshmi not on his left but on his right side. As is well known, only his consort or wife can occupy the left side of a male deity. Thus this distinction is quite noticeable that while in the temples the Goddess reposes at the left hand side of Lord Vishnu, in the Deewali idols and images Lakshmi occupies her seat right of Ganesh. Ganesh-Lakshmi's this combination is unique for no other god is ever depicted or worshipped with the spouse of some other god. Their joint image clearly indicates that their association was thought of much later than the association of Vishnu and Lakshmi.

7. लक्ष्मी देवी की प्रसिद्ध स्तुतियाँ, श्लोक, प्रार्थनाएं, आरती इत्यादि

(नागरी व रोमन लिपि में मूल पाठ एवम् हिन्दी-अंग्रेजी में अनुवाद सहित)

(i) महालक्ष्म्यष्टकम्

इन्द्र उवाच:

नमस्तेऽस्तु महामाये श्री पीठे सुरपूजिते ।
शङ्खचक्रगदाहस्ते महालक्ष्मि नमोऽस्तु ते ॥ १॥

इन्द्र बोले:– श्री पीठ पर स्थित और देवताओं से पूजित होनेवाली हे महामाये! तुम्हें नमस्कार है । हाथ में शङ्ख, चक्र और गदा धारण करनेवाली हे महालक्ष्मि! तुम्हें प्रणाम है ॥ १॥

नमस्ते गरुडारूढे कोलासुरभयङ्करि ।
सर्वपापहरे देवि महालक्ष्मि नमोऽस्तु ते ॥२॥

गरुड़ पर आरूढ़ हो कोलासुर को भय देनेवाली और समस्त पापों को हरनेवाली हे भगवति महालक्ष्मि! तुम्हें प्रणाम है ॥२॥

सर्वज्ञे सर्ववरदे सर्वदुष्टभयङ्करि ।
सर्वदुःखहरे देवि महालक्ष्मि नमोऽस्तु ते ॥३॥

7. Some Famous and Popular Hymns, Orisons, Ārtis etc., of Goddess Lakshmi

(With Their Romanised Text Versions and Hindi-English Translations)

(i) Eight Verses of Eulogy for Goddess Lakshmi

Indra Uvācha:

> Namastestu Mahāmaye Shreepeethe Surpoojite |
> Shankha Chakra gadā haste Mahalakshmi namostute ||1||

Indra said: O Grand Goddess, seated on the exalted pedestal and worshipped by the gods ! I bow to thee! O Mahālakshmi ! Weilding conch, chakra (discus) and mace in your hands ! I salute you ||1||

> Namaste Garudāroodhe Kolasurabhayankari |
> Sarva Pāp hare Devi, Mahālakshmi namostute ||2||

O Goddess Mahalakshmi ! Riding on Garuda, frightening the demon called Kolasur and remover of all sin, I bow to thee ||2||

> Sarvagye sarva-varade sarvadushtabhayankari |
> Sarvadukkhahare Devi Mahālakshmi namostute ||3||

सब कुछ जाननेवाली, सबको वर देने वाली, समस्त दुष्टों को भय देने वाली और सबके दु:खों को दूर करने वाली, हे देवि महालक्ष्मि! तुम्हें नमस्कार है ॥३॥

सिद्धिबुद्धिप्रदे देवि भुक्तिमुक्तिप्रदायिनि ।
मन्त्रपूते सदा देवि महालक्ष्मि नमोऽस्तु ते ॥४॥

सिद्धि, बुद्धि, भोग और मोक्ष देने वाली हे मन्त्रपूत भगवति महालक्ष्मि! तुम्हें सदा प्रणाम है ॥४॥

आद्यान्तरहिते देवि आद्यशक्ति महेश्वरि
योगजे योग सम्भूते महालक्ष्मि नमोऽस्तुते ॥५॥

हे देवि! हे आदि-अन्त-रहित आदिशक्ति ! हे महेश्वरि ! हे योग से प्रकट हुई भगवति महालक्ष्मि तुम्हें नमस्कार है ॥५॥

स्थूलसूक्ष्म महारौद्रे महाशक्ति महोदरे ।
महापापहरे देवि महालक्ष्मि नमोऽस्तुते ॥६॥

हे देवि! तुम स्थूल, सूक्ष्म एवं महारौद्ररूपिणी हो, महाशक्ति हो, महोदरा हो और बड़े-बड़े पापों का नाश करने वाली हो । हे देवि महालक्ष्मि! तुम्हें नमस्कार है ॥ ६॥

पद्मासनास्थिते देवि परब्रह्मस्वरूपिणि ।
परमेशि जगन्मातर्महालक्ष्मि नमोऽस्तु ते ॥७॥

हे कमल के आसन पर विराजमान परब्रह्मस्वरूपिणी देवि! हे परमेश्वरि! हे जगदम्ब! हे महालक्ष्मि! तुम्हें मेरा प्रणाम है ॥७॥

श्वेताम्बरधरे देवि नानालङ्कारभूषिते ।
जगत्स्थिते जगन्मातर्महालक्ष्मि नमोऽस्तुते ॥८॥

O Godess Mahalakshmi! You are Omniscient, you grant boons to all and frighten all the wicked! You are the remover of all sorrows, I bow to thee ||3||

> Siddhibuddhiprade Devi bhuktimuktipradāyani |
> Mantrapoote sadā devi Mahālakshmi namostute ||4||

O Great goddess Lakshmi! Purified by the Mantra, you grant to your devotees wisdom, capacities to attain perfection and indulge in enjoyment and you are the one who grants final emancipation to their souls or the Moksha ||4||

> Ādyāantarahite Devi Ādyashaktimaheshwari |
> Yogje yogasambhoote Mahālakshmi namostute ||5||

O Goddess, without any beginning or end, the Primal Power! O Grand Deity! Manifest only through the concentrated devotion! I bow to thee! ||5||

> Sthoolasookshma Mahāraudre Mahāshakti mahodare |
> Mahāpāphare Devi Mahālakshmi namostute ||6||

O Goddess! You are visibly manifest but also subtly existent, and you have terrible appearance! You are the primal power, having great capacity to end severest afflictions. O Great Goddess! I bow to thee! ||6||

> Padmāsanasthite Devi Parbrahmaswaroopini |
> Parameshi jagan mātar-Mahālakshmi namostute ||7||

Seated on the lotus flower, O manifest form of the Supreme Being! O Goddess! O Supreme Goddss! Mother of the World! O Mahālakshmi! I bow to thee! ||7||

> Shwetāmbar-dhare Devi nānālankara-bhooshite |
> Jagatisthite jaganmātar mahālakshmi namostute ||8||

हे देवि! तुम श्वेत वस्त्र धारण करने वाली और नाना प्रकार के आभूषणों से विभूषित हो। सम्पूर्ण जगत् में व्याप्त एवं अखिल लोक को जन्म देनेवाली हो। हे महालक्ष्मि! तुम्हें मेरा प्रणाम है ॥८॥

महालक्ष्म्यष्टकं स्तोत्रं य: पठेद्भक्तिमान्नर: ।
सर्वसिद्धिमवाप्नोति राज्यं प्राप्नोति सर्वदा ॥९॥

जो मनुष्य भक्तिपूर्वक इस महालक्ष्यष्टक स्तोत्र का सदा पाठ करता है, वह सारी सिद्धियों और राज्यवैभव को प्राप्त कर सकता है ॥९॥

एक काले पठेन्नित्यं महापापविनाशनम् ।
द्विकालं य: पठेन्नित्यं धनधान्यसमन्वित: ॥१०॥

जो प्रतिदिन एक समय पाठ करता है उसके बड़े-बड़े पापों का नाश हो जाता है। जो दो समय पाठ करता है वह धन धान्य से सम्पन्न होता है ॥१०॥

त्रिकालं य: पठेन्नित्यं महाशत्रुविनाशनम् ।
महालक्ष्मीर्भवेन्नित्यं प्रसन्ना वरदा शुभा ॥११॥

जो प्रतिदिन तीन काल (इस अष्टक का) पाठ करता है उसके महान शत्रुओं का नाश हो जाता है और उसके ऊपर कल्याण कारिणी वरदायिनी महालक्ष्मी सदा ही प्रसन्न होती है ॥११॥

O Goddess! You are clad in white clothes and decorated with many garments! You instinct the whole world by your presence and all the realms come into being by your grace. O Mahalakshmi! I bow to thee ||8||

> Mahālakshmyashtakam strotram yah pathedbhaktimānnarah |
> Sarvasiddhimavāpnoti rājyam prāpnoti sarvada ||9||

He who always reads this Mahalakshmyashtakam with devotion and concentration becomes eligible to attain all perfections and kingly opulence ||9||

> Ekakāle pathennityam mahāpāpavināshanam |
> Dwikālam yah pathennityam dhanadhanya samanvitah ||10||

He who reads it once daily has his severest sins destroyed. He who reads it twice daily gets all kinds of riches and wealth ||10||

> Trikālam yah pathennityam mahāshatruvinashanam |
> Mahalakshmeerbhavennityam prasanna varadā shubhā ||11||

He who reads it thrice daily not only has his most powerful enemies destroyed but ever remains the favourite of the auspicious—boon bestowing Grand Goddess Lakshmi ||11||

(ii) देव्या आरात्रिकम्

प्रवरातीरनिवासिनि निगमप्रतिपाद्ये
पारावारविहारिणि नारायणि हृद्ये ।
प्रपञ्चसारे जगदाधारे श्रीविद्ये
प्रपन्नपालननिरते मुनिवृन्दाराध्ये
जय देवि जय देवि जय मोहनरूपे
मामिह जननि समुद्धर पतितं भवकूपे ॥१॥

हे प्रवरानदीतीरवासिनी, वेदों से प्रतिपादित, क्षीरसागरविहारिणी, नारायणप्रिया, मनोहारिणी, संसार की सार और आधाररूपिणी, लक्ष्मी और विद्यारूपिणी, शरणागत की रक्षा में तत्पर, मुनिगणों से आराधित हे देवि! तुम्हारी जय हो, जय हो! हे मनोहर रूपवाली! तुम्हारी जय हो ! हे मातः! इस संसार कूप में पड़े हुए मेरा उद्धार करो ॥१॥

दिव्यसुधाकरवदने कुन्दोज्ज्वलरदने
पदनखनिर्जितमदने मधुकैटभकदने
विकसितपङ्कजनयने पन्नगपतिशयने
खगपतिवहने गहने सङ्कटवन दहने ॥ जय देवि०॥२॥

पूर्ण चन्द्र के समान दिव्यमुखवाली, कुन्दपुष्प के-से स्वच्छ दाँतों वाली, अपने पैरों की नख-ज्योति से मदन को पराजित करने वाली, मधुकैटभ का संहार करने वाली, प्रफुल्लित कमल-समान नेत्रोंवाली, शेषशायिनी, गरूडवाहिनी, दुराराध्या, संकटवन को भस्म करने वाली (हे देवि ! तुम्हारी जय हो, जय हो) ॥२॥

(ii) The Evening Invocation of the Goddess

Parvarāteeraniwāsini nigamapratipādye
 Parāvāravihārini nārāyani hridye
Prapanchasāre jagadādhāre Shree vidye
 Prapannapālananirate munivrindārādhye
Jai Devi jai devi jai mohan roope
 Māmiha janani samuddhara patitam bhavakoope ||1||

O Dweller on the bank of the river Pravarā; enunciated by the Vedas; reveller in the ocean of Milk; the beloved of Narayan (Vishnu); the enchantress; the root cause and base of the world; Lakshmi, the goddess; the embodiment of all knowledge; ever-ready to help the one seeking refuge in you; O Goddess, ever reverenced by the high seers and sages ! Victory to thee, Victory to thee ! O Comely visaged ! Victory to thee! O Mother: redeem me from this well of worldly existence. ||1||

Divyasudhākar-vadane kundojjwalaradane
 Padanakhanirjitamadane Madhu-kaitabha-kadane
Vikasita pankajanayane pannagapatishayane
 Khagpativahane gahane Sankatavana dahne || Jai Devi ||2||

O With a divine visage like the full moon; having teeth as white as the flower of kunda; brow-beating even the god of beauty merely by the radiance of your shining nails; the slayer of the demons Madhu and Kaitabh; having eyes like a fully bloomed lotus, lying on the bed made by the coiling serpent Shesh, rider of Garuda, difficult to please deity; the incinerator of the jungle of afflictions-O Goddess! Victory to thee, victory to thee ! ||2||

मञ्जीराङ्कितचरणे मणिमुक्ताभरणे
कञ्चुकिवक्षावरणे वक्त्राम्बुजधरणे ।
शक्रामयभयहरणे भूसुरसुखकरणे
करुणां कुरू मे शरणे गजनक्रोद्धरणे । जय देवि०॥३॥

चरणों में नूपुर धारण करनेवाली, मणि और मोतियों के आभूषण धारण करने वाली, चोली और वस्त्रों से सुसज्जित, कमलमुखी, इन्द्र की विघ्न-बाधाओं को दूर करने वाली, ब्राह्मणों के लिए आनन्ददायिनी, गज और ग्राह का उद्धार करने वाली हे देवि! मुझ शरणागत पर कृपा करो ।(हे देवि! तुम्हारी जय हो! जय हो! जय हो !!) ॥३॥

छित्वा राहुग्रीवां पासि त्वं विबुधान्
ददासि मृत्युमनिष्टं पीयूषं विबुधान् ।
विहरसि दानवऋद्धान समरे संसिद्धान्
मध्वमुनीश्वरवरदे पालय संसिद्धान । जय देवि ॥४॥

तुम राहु की ग्रीवा काट कर देवों की रक्षा करती हो, असुरों को उनकी इच्छा के विपरीत मृत्यु और देवताओं को अमृत देती हो, युद्ध कुशल और वीर दैत्यों से रण क्रीड़ा करने वाली हो । हे मध्वमुनीश्वर को वर देनेवाली ! भक्तों का पालन करो । (हे देवि! तुम्हारी जय हो, जय हो!) ॥४॥

80

Manjeerānkitacharane manimuktābharane
  Kanchukivastrāvarane vaktrāmbujadharane
Shakrāmayabhayaharane Bhoosurasukhakarane
  Karunām kuru me sharane gajanakroddharane
  || Jai Devi ...||3||

O Wearer of the tinkling bells in the feet, adorned with many ornaments embedded with pearls and gems; clad in beauteous breast band and other clothes; with a lotus like face; the destroyer of afflictions to Indra; bestowing bliss to the brahmans, the redeemer of the elephant from the Crocodile's clutches—O Goddess! Shed your grace on me deeming me to be seeking shelter under your protection ! (O Goddess ! victory to thee! Victory to thee) ||3||

  Chhitvā Rahugreevam pāsi tvam vibudhān
  Dadāsi mrityumanishtam peeyusham vibudhān
  Viharasi dānavariddhān samare samsiddhān
  Madhvamuneeshwar varade pālaya samsiddhan
  || jai Devi ...||4||

You had hacked off the head of Rahu to protect the gods; you bestow nectar to the gods but give death to the demons contrary to their desires; you are an expert warrior and browbeat the valiant demons in the war games ! O Bestower of the boon to the great sage Madhwa! Protect your devotees. [O Goddess ! victory to thee, victory to thee !] ||4||

(iii) श्री लक्ष्मी चालीसा

जय जय जय श्री लक्ष्मी, कीजइ कृपा अपार ।
दीजइ धन जन जानि निज, लीजइ शरण मँझार ॥

हे लक्ष्मी जी मैं आपकी जय-जय कार करता हूँ । आप मुझ पर अपार कृपा कीजिए—मुझे अपना भक्त जान कर अपनी शरण में लीजिए और धन-धान्य से सम्पन्न कीजिए ।

जयति जयति जगनिधिवती, भाग्यवती धनवन्ति ।
जय जय जलज विलासिनी घट-घट में विचरन्ति ॥

हे समस्त जगत की सम्पत्ति की स्वामिन ! हे धन और भाग्य की अधिष्ठात्री देवि ! मैं आपकी जय-जयकार करता हूँ । आप कमल पर विराजती हैं और समस्त जगत में विचरण करती रहती हैं ।

जय जय कमले हरि प्रिये, जलनिधि तनये अम्ब ।
विनवत 'सुन्दरदास' इक मान तेरा अवलम्ब ॥

हे कमला, हे विष्णु की प्रिय अर्द्धांगिनी, हे समुद्र की कन्या श्री अम्बे माता ! 'सुन्दरदास' आपकी विनती करता है क्योंकि उसका मात्र तू ही एक सहारा है ।

सब सुखदायिनी लक्ष्मी अम्बा ।
दीनन हित क्यों करति विलम्बा ॥१॥

हे समस्त सुख को देने वाली लक्ष्मी मैय्या ! आप मुझ जैसे दीनों पर अपनी कृपा करने में क्यों विलम्ब कर रही हैं ।

(iii) Forty Rhymes in the Honour of Goddess Lakshmi

Jai jai jai Shree Lakshmi, keejai kripā apār ।
Deejai dhan jan jāni nij, leejai sharan manjhār ॥

O Goddess Lakshmi! Victory to thee, victory to thee! Please shed your infinite grace upon me—deeming me to be your devotee seeking your shelter—and make me affluent with all kinds of riches.

Jayati jayati jagnidhavati, bhāgyawati dhanvanti ।
Jai jai jalaj vilasini, ghat-ghat men vicharanti ॥

O Mistress of all the riches of the world! O Goddess of fortune and finances! I raise victory slogans in your honour! Your seat is the lotus flower and you roam about all over the world!

Jai jai kamale Haripriye, jalanidhi tanaye amb ।
Vinavat 'Sunderdas' ik mān tera avalamb ॥

O Kamala! O Beloved Spouse of Lord Vishnu! O Daughter of the Ocean! O Mother of the World! 'Sunderdas' requests you to help him as he has no other shelter or support.

Sab sukhadāyani Lakshmi Amba ।
Deenan hit kyon Karati vilamba ॥1॥

O Mother Lakshmi, the bestower of all kinds of comforts to your devotees, why are you delaying in shedding your grace upon such a troubled and shelterless person like me?

तू त्रिभुवन तम नासनिहारी
हे जग्जननि विष्णु की प्यारी ॥२॥

हे माता! हे समस्त जगत की जननि और विष्णु की प्रिया! आप ही समस्त जगत का तम (त्रास व विपन्नता) का नाश करती हैं।

भेद तुम्हार न कोई पावत।
क्षण मँह सुख सम्पति उपजावत ॥३॥

आपका भेद कोई भी नहीं जान सका है कि आप कैसे क्षण मात्र में सारी सम्पत्ति व सुख (अपने भक्तों के लिए) उपलब्ध करा देती हैं।

पावत शेषादिक नहिं अंता
महिमा अनुपम अगम अनंता ॥४॥

समस्त ज्ञानी, मुनि तथा हजार मुखों वाले शेषनाग भी आपकी महिमा का अन्त नहीं जान पाए हैं। आपकी महिमा अनुपम है अगम है तथा उसका कोई ओर-छोर नहीं है।

मुकुट बीच शिशु चन्द विराजत
तीसर नयन भाल बिच साजत ॥५॥

आपके शीश पर मुकुट है और उसके बीच में नवोदित चन्द्रमा की छवि है। आपके मस्तक के मध्य तीसरा नयन भी सुशोभित है।

दिप-दिप दमके मणिन लरन की
सोहत चोली हरित वरन की ॥६॥

आपकी मणिपूरित लड़ें दीप्यमान हो रही हैं और आपकी चोली हरे रंग की है।

Tu tribhuvan tam nāsanihāri
Hey jagjjanani Vishnu ki pyāri ||2||

O Mother! O Mother of the World and darling of Lord Vishnu ! Only you destroy all darkness (of privation and affliction) of the entire world.

Bhed tumhār na koi pāvat |
Kshan manhi sukh sampati upjavat ||3||

None could ever fathom your glory as to how, in a trice, you procure every kind of wealth and riches (for your devotees).

Pāvat Sheshādik nahin antā
Mahimā anupam agam anantā ||4||

All the great seers, sages, the thousand mouthed serpent shesh could never fathom your glory which is ineffable, incomparable and endless.

Mukut beecha shishu chanda virājat
Teesar nayan bhāl bicha sājat ||5||

Your head is bedight with a crown having a nascent moon in the middle. A bright third eye also glows amidst your forehead.

Dip-dip damake manina laran ki
Sohat Choli harita baran ki ||6||

Your gem-studded laces are dazzling brightly and your upper garment is of green colour.

पुष्पराज हिय हार विराजत
लखि छवि सहस मदन मन लाजत ॥७॥

पुष्पराज (पुखराज) की मालाएं हृदय पर अत्यधिक शोभा को प्राप्त हो रही है—उनकी छवि देख कर सहस्रों कामदेवों का मन लज्जित हो जाता है (अर्थात् फीके पड़ जाते हैं)

फहरत अरुन रंग की सारी
मरकत मणि शुचि जड़ित किनारी ॥८॥

आपके दिव्य शरीर पर बाल-सूर्य की आभा के समान सारी सुशोभित है जिसकी शुभ मरकत मणिसे किनारी जड़ी हुई है ।

कटि कंकणि गुछित करघनियाँ
पद कमलन भाँकत पैंजनियां ॥९॥

आपकी कमर पर मणि-जड़ी हुई करधनी शोभित है और कमल के समान पाँवों पर पैंजनिया शोभायमान है ।

शोभा अमित तेज की खानी ।
लसित शस्त्र अष्टादस पानी ॥१०॥

आपकी सम्पूर्ण छवि अमित तेज की खान प्रतीत होती है और आपके अठारह हाथों में विभिन्न प्रकार के शस्त्र दमक रहे हैं ।

गदा-पद्म त्रिशूल-कृपानन ।
शंख चक्र राजत धनुबानन ॥११॥

(आपके हाथों में) गदा, कमल, त्रिशूल एवम कृपाण हैं । अन्य हाथ में शंख चक्र भी धनुष और बाणों के बीच में सुशोभित है ।

Pushparaj hiya hār virajat
Lakhi chavi sahas madan man lājat ||7||

The laces studded with the gem of flowers bedight your bosom supremely—looking to their beauty even the thousand Kāmdevas feel belittled.

Phaharat arun rang ki sāri
Markat mani shuchi jarita kināri ||8||

The raiment on your divine body is as radiant as the glow of the rising sun, having its border studded as though with the bright emeralds.

Kati kankani guchhit kardhaniyān
Pad-kamalan jhankat paijaniyān ||9||

The golden girdle round your waist has many gems studded and the glimpse of the beauteous ankle-bells is seen through the movement of your lotus feet.

Shobha amita tej ki khāni |
Lasita shastra asthtadas pāni ||10||

Your entire image is very dazzing as though it is the mine of all virtue shining like the gems. You have many radiant weapons in all of your eighteen hands.

Gadā-padma trishool kripānan
Shankha chakra rājat dhanu-bānan ||11||

You have the mace, the lotus, the trident and the dagger, the bow, the conch and the arrows in your hands.

वज्र कुण्डिका पाशु कुथारी ।
अति शुचि अक्षमाल कर धारी ।।१२।।

(आपके हाथों में) वज्र, कुण्डिका, पाशु और कुठारी शोभित है तथा अत्यन्त पवित्र अक्षमाला आपके हाथों में पड़ी हुई है ।

सुधा कलश रस हस्त विराजत ।
घन्टा विजय घनन् घन् बाजत ।।१३।।

आपके हाथों में अमृत घट रखा हुआ है और आपकी विजय का घंटा.... घनन-घन का शब्द करता हुआ अनवरत बना रहा है ।

मन उपजाति कथा सुखदाई ।
वेद पुरान सदा यश गाई ।।१४।।

अब मेरे मन में एक कथा की उत्पत्ति जन्म ले रही है जिसके बारे में वेद पुरानों सदा यशगान करते हैं ।

एक समय अस विधि भे वामा ।
मचिगे देवासुर संग्रामा ।।१५।।

एक समय विधाता ऐसा वाम (विपरीत) हुआ कि देवों और सुरों (देवताओं) का भयंकर संग्राम शुरू हो गया ।

सुर-असुरन मैँहि अति भयकारी ।
मच्यौ युद्ध तिहुँ लोक मँफारी ।।१६।।

और उनके (देवताओं तथा असुरों के) बीच ऐसा भयंकर युद्धा मचा कि तीनों लोक उस युद्ध की विभिषिका से आतंकित हो उठे थे ।

>Vajra kundika pāshu kuthāri
>Ati shuchi Akashāmāl kar dhāri ||12||

The thunderbolt, the cistern, the snoose, the axe and the beautiful rosary look comely in your hands.

>Sudhā-kalash ras hasta virajat
>Ghanta vijay ghanan ghan bājat ||13||

Your one hand holds the pitcher of nectar and the other a bell which constanlty sound to proclaim your victory.

>Man up jāti kathā sukhdāyee
>Ved-purān sada yash gāyee ||14||

Now I am reminded of an event which the Vedas and scriptures ever glorify.

>Ek samaya as vidhi bhe vāmā |
>Machige Devāsur sangrāmā ||15||

Once it so happened that owing to unfortunte spell of destiny, there was raged a terrible war between the gods and the demons.

>Sur-Asuran manhi ati bhayakāri |
>Machyo yuddha tihun lok manjhari ||16||

The war was so ferocious and so wide-ranging that all the three realms were afflicted by its devastations.

> विकट असुर तब निज भुजबल से
> सुरन्हि पराजित कीन्हों छल से ॥१७॥

तब असुरों ने अपनी मायावी शक्ति द्वारा देवताओं को छल से पराजित कर दिया । वे असुर बड़े विकट थे और उनको जीत पाना संभव नहीं था ।

> तब देवन जाइ करी गुहारी
> ब्रह्मा विष्णु और त्रिपुरारी ॥१८॥

तब देवताओं ने जाकर ब्रह्मा, विष्णु और त्रिपुरारी (शिव) से प्रार्थना की [कि किसी प्रकार उन्हें इन असुरों से बलशाली बनाना जाय ।

> उदधि विलोड़न युक्ति सुझाई
> पाय सुधा सुर लें अमराई ॥१९॥

तब उन्हें यह युक्ति सुझाई गई कि किसी प्रकार सिन्धु का विलोड़न कर उससे अमृत प्राप्त किया जाए जिससे देवता लोग अमर हो सकें ।

> सुधा हेतू दानव अकुलाए
> देवन सँग निज हाथ बटाए ॥२०॥

अमृत प्राप्ति की युक्ति सुन कर दानव भी आकुल हो गए और देवताओं के साथ उदधि विलोड़न हेतु सहयोग देने के लिए राजी हो गए ।

> क्षीर-सिन्धु जब विष्णु मथायो
> चौदह रत्न सिन्धु में पायो ॥२१॥

इस प्रकार जब विष्णु के आदेश पर देवता और दानवों ने क्षीर-सिन्धु का मन्थन किया तो उस में से चौदह रत्न निकले ।

> Vikat asur tab nij bhujabal se
> Suranhi parājit keenhon chhal se ||17||

Then those grisly demons managed to defeat the gods by their black-magical tricks; the demons appeared invincible owing to their might.

> Tab devan Jāi kari guhāri
> Brahmā Vishnu aur tripurāri ||18||

Then the gods fled and requested succour from the Supreme Gods of Trinity, Brahma, Vishnu and Shiv.

> Udadhi-vilorhan yukti sujhāyee
> Pāya sudhā sur len amarāyee ||19||

The gods were, then, asked to get the ocean churned. This churning was likely to bring out nectar, imbibing which the gods were sure to become immortal.

> Sudha-hetu dānav akulāye
> Devan sang nij hāth batāye ||20||

Learning about the nectar the demons were also attracted to the project and readily agreed to cooperate with the gods.

> Ksheer sindhu jab Vishnu mathāyo
> Chaudaha ratna Sindhu men pāyo ||21||

Then on the advice of Vishnu when the gods and demons jointly churned the ocean, there emerged fourteen gems.

चौदह रत्न में तुम सुखरासी।
विष्णु संग पायो अविनासी॥२२॥

उन चौदहों रत्न में से एक, हे समस्त सुखों की राशि लक्ष्मी मैय्या, आप भी एक थीं । बाहर आते ही अपने सदा-सर्वदा के लिए विष्णु का वरण कर दिया ।

जो जो जन्म जहाँ प्रभु लीन्हा ।
रूप बदल तहँ सेवा कीन्हा ॥२३॥

फिर तो जहाँ-जहाँ विष्णु ने अवतार लिया, आप भी विभिन्न रूपों में प्रकट होकर निरंतर उनके साथ रहीं और उनकी सेवा करती रहीं ॥

स्वयं विष्णु जहाँ नर-तन धारा ।
लीन्हेहु अवधपुरी अवतारा ॥२४॥

जब भगवान विष्णु ने मनुष्य का शरीर धारण कर अवधपुरी में अवतार लिया (श्री राम के रूप में)—

तब तुम प्रकट जनक पुर माहीं ।
सेवा कियो हृदय पुलकाहीं ॥२५॥

तब, हे माता लक्ष्मी! आप ने जनक पुर में (सीता के रूप में) जन्म लिया और श्री राम को पुनः पतिरूप पाकर पुलकित हुई

तुम सम प्रबल शक्ति नहिं आनी ।
कहँ तक महिमा कहौं बखानी ॥२६॥

आपकी प्रबल शक्ति की कोई सीमा नहीं है—आपकी महिमा इतनी विशाल है कि मैं उसका कब तक वर्णन कर सकता हूँ। (अर्थात् वह वर्णनातीत है)

Chaudah Ratna men tum sukhrāsi
Vishnu sang pāyo Avināsi ||22||

Out of those fourteen gems, O Mine of All Happiness, O Mother Lakshmi ! You were one of them. Coming out of the ocean you chose Lord Vishnu's companionship for ever.

Jo jo janma jahan prabhu leenhā
Roop badal tahan sewa keenhā ||23||

Then after, wherever Vishnu incarnated himself you followed Him changing your form accordingly, and rendered him devoted service.

Swayan Vishnu jahan nar-tan dhārā
Leenehu Avadhpuri avataarā ||24||

When Lord Vishnu Chose to incarnate himself in human form in Avadhpuri (as Lord Rām)—

Tab tum prakat janakpur mānheen
Sewa kiyo hridaya pulkāheen ||25||

Then O Mother Lakshmi! You took birth in Janakpur (in the form of Sita) and was delighted to have received Lord Ram as your husband ||25||

Tum sum prabal shakti nahin ānee |
Kahan tak Mahimā kahon bakhānee ||26||

There is no end to your immense power—your glory is so great that I just cannot describe it fully.

मन क्रम वचन करै सेवकाई ।
मन इच्छित वांछित फल पाई ॥२७॥

जो लक्ष्मी जी की मन, वचन और कर्म से सेवा करता है उसे मन वांछित फल प्राप्त हो जाता है ।

त्राहि-त्राहि जै दु:ख निवारिणि ।
त्रिविध ताप भव बन्धन हारिणि ॥२८॥

हे माता! मैं त्राहि-त्राहि कर रहा हूँ । आप तुरन्त आकर मेरे दु:खों का निवारण करें । हे दु:ख निवारण करने वाली माता आप तीनों प्रकार के (दैविक, दैहिक और भौतिक) तापों का शमन कर संसार के समस्त कष्टों को दूर करने में सक्षम हैं ।

जो यह पढ़े और पढ़वावै ।
ध्यान लगाकर सुनै सुनावै ॥२९॥
ताकों कोई न रोग सतावै ।
पुत्र-आदि धन सम्पति पावै ॥३०॥

जो कोई (व्यक्ति) इस (चालीसा) को ध्यान लगा कर पढ़ता या सुनता है उसे कभी कोई रोग नही सताता है और वह पुत्र-आदि धन सम्पत्ति से परिपूर्ण रहता है ।

पाठ करै जो दिन चालीसा ।
ता पर कृपा करै जगदीसा ॥३१॥

जो इस पाठ को चालीस दिनों तक करता या करवाता है उस पर जगदीश भगवान विष्णु की भी तुरंत कृपा हो जाती है ।

Man Krama Vachan karei sevakāee
Man ichhita vānchhit phal pāyee ||27||

He who renders devoted service to Goddess Lakshmi by his deed, word and action gets his desired boon.

Trāhi Trāhi jai dukkha niwārini |
Trividha tāp bhav bandhan hārini ||28||

O Mother ! I am severely distressed and cry for succour. Please come immediately and redeem me from these afflictions. O Mother who quickly dispels all afflictions, you are quite capable of removing all the three types (physical, spiritual and mental) of sorrow.

Jo yeha padhei aur padhavāve |
Dhyan lagā kar sunei sunave ||29||
Tākon koi na rog satāve
Putra-ādi dhan sampati pāve ||30||

He who reads or listens to this (Chāleesā) with total devotion and concentration does not ever get afflicted with any disease and always remains affluent with all kinds of riches.

Pāth karei jo din Chāleesā |
Tā par kripā karen Jagdeesā ||31||

He who reads or listens to this Chāleesā for forty days becomes also the favourite of Lord Vishnu and gets the benefit of his grace immediately.

सुख-सम्पत्ति बहुतायत पावै ।
कमी नहीं काहूँ की आवै ॥३२॥

उसे सुख और सम्पत्ति की बहुतायत से प्राप्ति होती है और कभी किसी प्रकार का अभाव नहीं खलता ।

करि विश्वास करै व्रत नेमा ।
होय सिद्धि उपजे उर प्रेमा ॥३३॥

जो पूर्ण विश्वास के साथ पूरे व्रत-नियम से इस (चालीसा) का पाठ करता है उसकी मनचाही सिद्धि प्राप्त हो जाती है और उसके हृदय में (माता लक्ष्मी के प्रति स्वाभाविक प्रेम उभरता है)

जय-जय-जय-जय लक्ष्मी माता ।
तुम्हरी कृपा दीन धन पाता ॥३४॥

हे माता लक्ष्मी आपकी जय हो, जय हो । आपकी कृपा से ही दीन-हीन व्यक्ति भी धन-धान्य से सम्पन्न हो जाता है ।

जय-जय भक्ति जननि जगदम्बा ।
सब की तुम हीं हौ अवलम्बा ॥३५॥

हे भक्ति की जननी, लक्ष्मी मैया! आप ही जगत की माता हैं और हम सब की तो आप ही एक मात्र सहारा हो ।

तुम्हरौ तेज प्रबल जग माहीं ।
तुम सम कोउ दयालहु नाहीं ॥३६॥

हे लक्ष्मी मैया! आप का समस्त जगत में प्रबल तेज (अर्थात्) प्रताप है और आपके समान कोई अन्य इतना दयालु भी नहीं है ।

> Sukh-sampati bahutāyat pāve |
> Kamee nahin kāhu kee āve ||32||

He gets immense riches and happiness and never suffers privations of any kind.

> Kari Vishwās karei vrata nemā |
> Hoya siddhi upaje ur premā ||33||

He who reads this Chāleesā with full faith, devotion and proper rituals gets the desired perfection and his heart gets replete with natural love (for the goddess).

> Jai jai jai jai Lakshmi Māta |
> Tumhari kripa deena dhan pāta ||34||

Victory to thee, O Mother Lakshmi ! It is only by your grace that even a resourceless, miserable pauper also becomes supremely rich and gets all kinds of wealth.

> Jai jai bhakti janani Jagdambā |
> Sab kee tum heen hau avalambā ||35||

O Mother of all devotion, Goddess Lakshmi ! You are the mother of the entire world and you are the sole shelter for the distressed and destitute persons like we are.

> Tumhro tej prabal jag mānheen |
> Tum sum kou dayalahu nāheen ||36||

O Mother Goddess! No one in the whole world is as brilliant and powerful as you are and no one is more kind hearted either.

मैं अनाथ मेरी सुधि लीजै ।
संकट काट भक्ति मोहि दीजै ॥३७॥

हे माता मैं अनाथ अर्थात् आश्रय रहित हूँ । अब आप शीघ्र मुझ पर कृपा कीजिए और मेरे संकटों का निवारण कर अपने श्री चरणों में मुझे अविचल भक्ति दीजिए ।

उठिके प्रात करत असनाना ।
जो कछु बनै करै सो दाना ॥३८॥

भक्त को चाहिए कि (अष्टमी तिथि को) प्रातः उठ कर स्नानादि से निवृत्त होकर जो कुछ बन पड़े उसका दान दे ।

सोलह दिन पूजा विधि करहीं ।
आश्विन कृष्ण जो अष्टमि परहीं ॥३९॥

उस अष्टमी (अश्विन कृष्ण पक्ष की) से जो लक्ष्मी माता की सोलह दिन पूरे विधि-विधान से पूजा करता है —

ताकर सब छूटै दुख दावा ।
सो जन सुख-सम्पत्ति नित पावा ॥४०॥

उस व्यक्ति को हर प्रकार के संकट-दुःख के दावानल (अर्थात् तपन) से सदैव के लिए मुक्ति मिल जाती है और वह सुख-सम्पत्ति से निरंतर भरा-पूरा रहता है ।

Mein anāth meree sudhi leejai |
Sankat kāt bhakti mohi deejai ||37||

O Mother ! I have no support from any one nor any shelter. Kindly dispel my distress and provide me unwavering devotion to your holy feet.

Uthike prāta karat asanānā |
Jo kacchu banei karei so dānā ||38||

The devotee should (on the eighth day, specially of the dark fortnight of the month of Aashwani) get up early in the morning, take his bath and then give alms according to his capacity.

Solaha din pooja vidhi karaheen |
Aashwani krishna jo ashtami paraheen ||39||

He who on the eighth day of the Aashwani month's dark fortnight (around Sept. end or Oct. beginning) starts worship of Lakshmi with full rituals and continues for full sixteen days—

Tākar sab chhootei dukh dāvā |
So jan sukh-sampati nita pāvā ||40||

—Gets final release from all worldly afflictions and fires and he ever remains happy, healthy, rich and prosperous.

(iv) श्री लक्ष्मी जी की आरती

जय लक्ष्मी माता, मैय्या जय लक्ष्मी माता
तुमको निसिदिन सेवत, हर हरि औ धाता।
  जय लक्ष्मी माता!

ब्रह्मानी, रुद्रानी कमला तू ही जगमाता
सूर्य चन्द्रमा ध्यावत, नारद रिषि गाता
  जय लक्ष्मी माता!

तेरो रूप निरंतर सुख सम्पति दाता
जो कोई तुमको ध्यावत, धन-सिद्धि पाता।
  जय लक्ष्मी माता!

जिस घर में तू रहती, सब सदगुण आता
कर न सके जो कर ले, मन नहीं घबड़ाता
  जय लक्ष्मी माता!

तुम बिन यज्ञ न होवे, वस्त्र न कोई पाता।
खान पान का वैभव तुम ही से आता।
  जय लक्ष्मी माता!

शुभ गुन मन्दिरा सुन्दर क्षीरोदधि जाता
रत्न चतुर्देश तुम्हीं, कोई नहीं पाता
  जय लक्ष्मी माता!

आरती लक्ष्मी जी की जो कोई नर गाता
उर आनन्द उमग अति, पाप उतर जाता
  जय लक्ष्मी माता!

अर्थ: हे लक्ष्मी माता तुम्हारी जय हो, जय हो! तुम्हारी वन्दना दिनों रात स्वयं शिव, विष्णु और विधाता ब्रह्मा भी करते रहते हैं। हे लक्ष्मी माता, तुम्हारी जय हो! तुम ही जगदम्बा हो, तुम्हें ही ब्रह्माणी, रुद्राणी और कमला के नाम से भी जाना जाता है, तथा सूर्य चन्द्र आपका ही ध्यान करते हैं और नारद सदृश देवर्षि भी आप की महिमा का गुणगान करते रहते हैं। आपके रूप का ध्यान निरंतर सुख-सम्पत्ति देने वाला है और जो कोई आपकी पूजा करता है वह मन चाहा धन और सिद्धि प्राप्त कर लेता है। हे लक्ष्मी मैय्या! आपकी जय हो।

(iv) Ārti of Goddess Lakshmi

Jai Lakshmi Māta, Maiyya jai Lakshmi Māta
Tumko nisadin sevat, Hara, Hari au, Dhātā
            Jai Lakshmi Māta !
Brahmāni, Rudrāni, Kamala tu hee jagmāta
Surya Chandramā dhyāvat, Nārad Rishi gāta
            Jai Lakshmi Māta !
Tero roop nirantar sukh sampati dātā
Jo koi tumko dhyāvat, dhan-siddhi pāta
            Jai Lakshmi Māta !
Jis ghar men tu rahati, sab sadgun ātā
kara na sake jo kar ley, man nahin ghabrhātā
            Jai Lakshmi Māta !
Tum bin yagya na hove, vastra na koi pātā
Khān pān kā vaibhava tum hee se ātā
            Jai Lakshmi Māta !
Shubha gun mandir sundar, ksheerodadhijātā
Ratna Chaturdash tumheen, koi nahin pātā
            Jai Lakshmi Māta !
Ārti Lakshmi jee kee jo koi nar gātā
Ur ānanda umaga ati, pāp utar jātā
            Jai Lakshmi Māta !

Meaning: O Mother Lakshmi, victory to thee, victory to thee! Even Shiv, Vishnu and Brahma ever reverence you day and night! Victory to thee, Mother Lakshmi! You are the mother of the world, and you are also famous as Rudrāni, Brahmāni and Kamalā. Even all the luminaries like the Sun and the Moon (deities) ever worship you devotedly and divine sage Nārad ever sings your great glory. The devoted worship of yours surely bestows all kind of riches and happiness and he who worships you

—जिस घर में आपका निवास होता है वहाँ सारे सद्गुण स्वंय ही आ जाते हैं और आपकी कृपा से असंभव कार्य करने में भी आपका भक्त सक्षम हो जाता है—वह बगैर घबड़ाए बड़े से बड़ा काम भी कर डालता है । आपकी कृपा के बगैर न कोई यज्ञ संभव है न समृद्धि-सारा वैभव और खान पान का ऐश्वर्य आपकी कृपा से ही प्राप्त हो पाता है । हे दूध के समुद्र की जायी कन्या! आप समस्त शुभ गुणों की खान हैं ! आपकी कृपा से ही देवतागण समुद्र से चौदह रत्नों की प्राप्ति कर पाए थे । वस्तुत: वह सारे चौदह रत्न आप स्वयं ही हैं । हे लक्ष्मी माता,आपकी जय हो । लक्ष्मी जी की यह आरती जो कोई भक्ति भाव से गाता है उसका हृदय आनन्द से ओत-प्रोत हो जाता है और उसके सारे पाप स्वंय ही नष्ट हो जाते हैं । हे लक्ष्मी मैय्या! आपकी जय हो!

इति

—with full faith in his heart gets the desired boon and attains perfection. O Mother Goddess! All virtues are attracted to the house you dwell in and by your grace one accomplishes even that mission whose very thought used to give one fright. Without your grace it is impossible to accomplish any yagya or big mission or get any prosperity; all affluence and even sensual pleasures are dependent upon your grace only. O Daughter of the Ocean of Milk! You are the mine of all virtues. It was only your grace which enabled the gods to churn out the Fourteen Gems. Victory to thee! Mother Lakshmi. He who sings this Ārti with total faith and devotion gets bliss in his heart and peace in his mind as his all sins get destroyed automatically. Victory to thee, Mother Lakshmi! Victory to thee!!

Other Valuable Books

Great Epics of India: Purana in 19 Vols. / *Bibek Debroy & Dipavali Debroy*

- *Brahma Purana
- *Vishnu Purana
- *Bhagavata Purana
- *Markandeya Purana
- *Bhavishya Purana
- *Linga Purana
- *Skanda Purana
- *Vamana Purana
- *Matsya Purana
- *Brahmanda Purana
- *Padma Purana
- *Shiva Purana
- *Narada Purana
- *Agni Purana
- *Brahmavaivarta Purana
- *Varaha Purana
- *Kurma Purana
- *Garuda Purana
- *Vayu Purana

(P.B.) Rs. 25 (each)

Great Epics of India: Veda in 4 Vols. / *Bibek Debroy & Dipavali Debroy*

- *Rig Veda
- *Sama Veda
- *Yajur Veda
- *Atharva Veda

(P.B.) Rs. 20 (each)